LEADERS OF THE CARIBBEAN

EXPLORING EFFECTIVE LEADERSHIP PRACTICES
THROUGH POPULAR CULTURE

Series editor: Michael J. Urick

The aim of this series is to examine modern and innovative business theories and methods via relatable popular cultural themes. The books will provide academically rigorous and credible applications and solutions to practitioners and upper level business students, in a format designed to be highly engaging and effective.

Titles in Exploring Effective Leadership Practices through Popular Culture

A Manager's Guide to Using the Force: Leadership Lessons from a Galaxy Far Far Away
Michael J. Urick

Leadership in Middle Earth: Theories and Applications for Organizations
Michael J. Urick

Leadership Insights for Wizards and Witches
Aditya Simha

Leaders Assemble! Leadership in the MCU
Gordon B. Schmidt and Sy Islam

Bend the Knee or Seize the Throne: Leadership Lessons from the Seven Kingdoms
Nathan Tong and Michael J. Urick

Courageous Companions: Followership in Doctor Who
Kimberly Yost

Against All Odds: Leadership and the Handmaid's Tale
Cristina de Mello e Souza Wildermuth

Leadership Lessons from the Kardashians: Bodies, Emotions, Success
Brigitte Biehl

Elements of Leadership: Lessons from Avatar the Last Airbender
Sy Islam and Gordon B. Schmidt

Forthcoming

Swift Leadership: A Taylor-made Approach to Influence and Decision Making
Mariah Yates and Michael J. Urick

Slaying the Vampires, Werewolves and Demons of Ineffective Leadership
Aditya Simha

LEADERS OF THE CARIBBEAN

Lead by the Code

By

Pelin Kohn
Community College of Vermont, USA

and

Michael J. Urick
Saint Vincent College, USA

emerald
PUBLISHING

United Kingdom – North America – Japan
India – Malaysia – China

Emerald Publishing Limited
Emerald Publishing, Floor 5, Northspring, 21-23 Wellington Street, Leeds LS1 4DL.

First edition 2025

Reprints and permissions service
Contact: permissions@emeraldinsight.com

British Library Cataloguing in Publication Data
A catalog record for this book is available from the British Library

ISBN: 978-1-83797-560-0 (Print)
ISBN: 978-1-83797-557-0 (Online)
ISBN: 978-1-83797-559-4 (Epub)

INVESTOR IN PEOPLE

I moved to the USA with my family seven years ago, and my journey of recreating my personal and professional life began as an explorer setting sail into uncharted waters, facing unknown challenges with courage and resilience. I dedicate this book to my children Alara and Arda, who have provided me with unwavering support and strength during this journey.

—Kohn

For the past 25 years, in addition to my day job, I have played music in bands semi-professionally and have had the opportunity to travel around the USA. At one point, I was struck that playing in and leading a band is very much like being a part of a crew of pirates. The crew members/players may come and go, but the music (i.e., the treasure) remains a constant quest. Sure, there are mutinies from time to time, but I have found that all of the concepts we address in this book apply to running a band (in addition to other types of organizations). I have found that the chapters on trust and communication especially apply. This book is dedicated to all of the musicians that I have played with over the years – you are like my crew of pirates.

—Urick

CONTENTS

About the Author   xv

Acknowledgments   xix

1   Introduction   1

    Charting the Course of Leadership Through the High Seas   1
    Characteristics of Effective Leadership   1
    The Importance of Continuous Learning in Leadership   3

2   The Captain's Code   7

    Leadership Strategies from the Caribbean   7
    Theories of Leadership in a Nutshell   7
        Situational Leadership Theories   8
        Servant Leadership Theory   8
        Authentic Leadership Theory   8
        Transactional Leadership Theory   9
        Relational Leadership Theory   9
    Captain Jack Sparrow: Transformational Leadership   9
    Captain Hector Barbossa: Transformational Leadership   11
    Will Turner: Servant Leadership   12
    Elizabeth Swann: Situational Leadership   14
    Tia Dalma: Authentic Leadership   16
    Davy Jones: Transactional Leadership   17
    Mr. Gibbs: Relational Leadership   18
    Summary   19

3 Building Trust Among a Crew   21

   Types of Trust   21
   Importance of Trust   23
   Breaking Trust   25
   Summary   26

4 Breaking Down Inequalities   27

   Social Construction Theory   27
   Elizabeth Swann: Challenging Traditional Gender Roles   28
   Tia Dalma/Calypso: Overcoming Objectification
       and Asserting Power   29
   Discussion on Gender and Gender Inequality in
       the Context of the Pirates of the Caribbean Series 29
       Challenging Traditional Gender Roles   30
       Asserting Agency and Power   30
       Building Engagement Through Representation   31
   Examining the Theory of Gender and Power in Light
       of the "Pirates of the Caribbean" Series   33
   A Feminist Political Ecology   34
   Summary   37

5 No Two Pirates are Alike   39

   Team Management Systems Model   40
   Social Exchange Theory   42
   Maslow's Hierarchy of Needs   42
   Navigating Maslow's Hierarchy of Needs with Pirates   43
       *Physiological Needs: Satisfying the Cravings of
           the Soul*   44
       Safety Needs: Balancing on the Edge of Uncertainty 45
       *Belongings and Love Needs: Finding
           Companionship in the Midst of Chaos*   46
       Esteem Needs: Dueling for Reputation and Respect 47
       *Self-actualization: Embracing the Freedom of
           Self-expression*   48
   Embracing Imperfections: Lessons from the Pirates   51
       Lesson 1: Relatability Through Vulnerability   51
       Lesson 2: Innovation and Creativity   51
       Lesson 3: Authenticity and Trust   52
       Lesson 4: Resilience and Growth   52

      Lesson 5: Building Diverse and Complementary Teams 52
      Lesson 6: Empathy and Understanding 53
   Summary 53

6 Learning How to Parley 55

   What is Parley? 55
   Historical Parleys 56
   Relationship to Negotiation 56
   Communication Type and Style 58
   Summary 60

7 Letting Your Compass Guide You 61

   True North: Values and Goals 61
   Understand What You Care About 62
   Motivation and Goal Setting Theory 63
   Summary 64

8 There Can Only Be One Captain 67

   Navigating Leadership Dynamics 68
      Embrace Competence and Expertise 69
      Balance Confidence and Humility 70
      Foster a Culture of Trust and Communication 71
      Be Accountable and Transparent 72
      Delegate Authority and Empower Your Crew 73
      Address Issues Early On 74
      Respect and Adapt to Change 75
   Embrace Diverse Ideas 77
      Unethical Leadership: The Path to Downfall 78
      The Dangers of Leader Isolation 79
      Charismatic Leadership: A Double-edged Sword 79
   Summary 80

9 Part of the Crew, Part of the Ship 81

   Fair Compensation 81
   Equity Theory 82
   Effective Problem-solving 83
   Effective Communication 86
   Summary 88

10 Tides of Change   91

  Systems Theory   91
     Risk Management in Systems Theory   92
     Understanding Interdependencies   92
     Identifying Systemic Risks   93
     Developing Comprehensive Strategies   93
     Protecting Organizational Assets and Reputation   94
     Enhancing Decision-making   94
     Fostering a Culture of Resilience and Agility   94
     Building Trust and Confidence   95
  Essential Leadership Skills for
     Effective Risk Management   95
     *Analytical Thinking: Problem Identification
        and Information Analysis*   95
     *Decision-making: Risk Assessment and
        Strategic Choices*   96
     Communication: Persuasion and Negotiation   97
     Agility: Adaptability and Flexibility   98
     Problem-solving: Creative and Critical Thinking   100
  Summary   101

11 Sailing into the Future   103

  Strategic Leadership Theory and Its Relation to
     Strategic Planning   104
  Strategic Planning Steps   105
     Preparation   105
     Adaptive Strategies   106
     Effective Execution   107
     Continuous Learning   108
  Summary   110

12 Stormy Seas   111

  Visionary Leadership   111
  Elements of Visionary Leadership in Crisis Management   111
     Adaptability and Flexibility   112
     Inspiration and Motivation   112
     Strategic Thinking and Innovation   112
     Resilience and Persistence   112
     Crisis Management   113

Leadership Strategies to Manage Crisis   113
    Rapid Assessment and Decision-making   113
    Communication and Coordination   113
    Adaptability and Flexibility   114
    Staying Calm Under Pressure   114
    Leading Through Uncertainty   114
    Learning and Reflection   115
Essential Leadership Qualities During Crises   115
    Quick Thinking and Adaptability   116
    Focus and Adaptation in Chaos   116
    Leveraging Diverse Strengths   116
    Balancing Short-term and Long-term Goals   117
    Being Resourceful and Adaptative   117
Summary   118

13 Conclusion   121

The Pirate's Legacy in 21st-century Leadership   121
Summary   124

Appendix 1: Pirates of the Caribbean Characters   125

Appendix 2: Pirates of the Caribbean Movies   127

References   129

ABOUT THE AUTHORS

Pelin Kohn is an elected City Councilor in Montpelier, Vermont, and a Leadership Educator. She intertwines 20+ years of executive coaching with competence-based leadership skills to make an impact on the community. She works for the Community College of Vermont (CCV). She orchestrated multidisciplinary partnerships as the Leadership Program Chair and Founding Director of the Center for Leadership in a senior military college, where she developed their Leadership Program, a nationally accredited Bachelor of Science in Leadership major with 12 new university courses where students gain a global leadership perspective. She is an inspiration for immigrant women in higher education. She is a distinguished fellow at the HERS Leadership Institute and a member of Vermont Women in Higher Education's executive board. She was selected as a fellow at The Snelling Center for Government's Vermont Leadership Institute to develop skills toward transformative change through collaborative leadership across sectors. She is always building a stronger toolkit to support her community.

She has a significant impact on civic issues. As an elected City Councilor, she works with fellow decision-makers to make a more diverse, sustainable, and efficient future for Montpelier, Vermont. She makes her constituents' voices heard more through public engagement projects such as community meetings. A strength of hers is solving local problems with a global mindset, a skill she developed through the Global Leadership Program for the Vermont Council on World Affairs. As an advocate for organizations such as the League of Women Voters of Vermont and non-profit ORCA Media, she shows her commitment to unity and diversity. Her new video program for ORCA, Leading with Purpose, explores the lives and leadership styles of Vermont's most impactful people. Through her EmergeVT fellowship, a program that fosters political leadership in women, she demonstrates her commitment to achieving a more inclusive political landscape.

Before moving to the USA, executive coach Pelin Kohn shaped leaders at global brands such as Bosch, British Petroleum, Ford, Hyundai, and

Turkish Airlines. Her leadership coaching transcends roles, resonating with the inner motivations of emerging and established leaders at all levels and backgrounds.

She is a sought-after keynote speaker who connects with people through storytelling. She offers a variety of leadership advancement programs that leave audiences inspired and better equipped to handle leadership challenges. Furthermore, she has written a book entitled "*Elevating Leadership: Innovative Teaching Methods to Develop Future Leaders.*"

She has a PhD in Educational Sciences, Administration, and Planning from Middle East Technical University in Turkey. She has a Master of Arts in Educational Sciences and History Teaching and a Bachelor of Arts in International Relations from Bilkent University. She holds a Certificate in Strategic Foresight from the University of Houston, a Diversity, Equity, and Inclusion Certificate from Cornell University, and a Certification in Creative Drama from American Catholic University. She is currently completing her MBA at Norwich University.

Embark on a journey of leadership, inspiration, and boundless possibilities with her. Follow her @PelinKohn and discover more at www.pelinkohn.com

Michael J. Urick is Dean of the Alex G. McKenna School of Business, Economics, and Government at Saint Vincent College in Latrobe, Pennsylvania, USA, as well as a Professor of Management and Operational Excellence.

He received his PhD in Management (Organizational Behavior focus) from the University of Cincinnati. His MBA (focused in Human Resources Management) and MS (in Leadership and Business Ethics) are both from Duquesne University in Pittsburgh and his Bachelor's degree in Accounting with Management and English minors is from Saint Vincent College. He has taught undergraduate and graduate courses related to organizational behavior, human resources, communication, conflict, organizational culture, operations, and research methods. His research has been widely cited in academic publications as well as in news media outlets such as the Wall Street Journal and the BBC.

The Master of Science in Management: Operational Excellence program at Saint Vincent, which he directed for nearly 10 years prior to his role as Dean, focuses on providing aspiring leaders with cutting edge management techniques to effectively solve the problem, minimize waste, and continuously improve their organizations. Under his directorship, the program was consistently ranked as a "Top 50 Best Value Master's in Management" program by Value Colleges and as a "Top Online Non-MBA Business Graduate Degree" by US News and World Report.

He is Six Sigma Green Belt Certified, Diversity Management Certified, a Certified Conflict Manager, Project Management Essentials Certified, and MBTI Certified and is also certified through the Society for Human Resource Management as well as the True Lean program at the University of Kentucky. He is the recipient of an "Excellence in Teaching" award from the Lindner College of Business at the University of Cincinnati, the "Quentin Schaut Faculty Award" from Saint Vincent College, and a "Teaching Excellence" award from the Accreditation Council for Business Schools and Programs among other pedagogical honors. Internationally, he was also recognized by the Institute for Supply Management as a "Person of the Year" in the learning and education category.

He is an Associate Editor of the Journal of Leadership and Management based in Poland, the North American Associate Editor of the Measuring Business Excellence journal, and on the editorial board of Management Teaching Review. He is also the Editor for the "Exploring Effective Leadership Practices through Popular Culture" book series from Emerald Publishing.

His research interests include leadership, conflict, and identity in the workplace. Much of his work focuses on issues related to intergenerational phenomena within organizations. He also often examines how popular culture can be used to advance organizational behavior theory. In addition to authoring or co-authoring over 50 publications including multiple books and peer-reviewed articles, he has regularly presented at academic and practitioner international meetings such as the Academy of Management, Society for Industrial and Organizational Psychology, and Institute for Supply Management conferences. He is a regular speaker on age-related issues in the workplace throughout the USA and internationally (having presented on four continents including presentations at the University of Oxford in the UK) and served as a consultant on issues related to workplace interactions, organizational culture, and ethics for various organizations. He has served as a reviewer for a variety of academic publications including the *Journal of Intergenerational Relationships, Journal of Social Psychology, Journal of Organizational Behavior*, and *Journal of Family Issues* as well as the *Organizational Behavior and Human Resources* divisions of the Academy of Management Annual Meeting in addition to other conferences.

Professionally, he has served on the boards of ISM-Pittsburgh (in various roles including President) and the Westmoreland Arts and Heritage Festival (a top-rated community event). He has also served on the Westmoreland Human Resources Association (a regional SHRM chapter) board in various positions including Vice President. Prior to academia, he worked in a variety of roles related to auditing, utilities, environmental issues, and training and development. Through these experiences, he became fascinated with interactions in the workplace and how they might be improved which has influenced his academic career.

For fun, he enjoys music and, since 1998, has been a semi-professional jazz musician and toured through over a dozen US states while releasing multiple recordings with various ensembles.

ACKNOWLEDGMENTS

Writing this book has been a remarkable journey, much like the adventurous tales of the pirates that inspired it. I am deeply grateful to those who have supported and guided me along the way.

I would like to thank my family for their unconditional support and encouragement. Moving to the USA seven years ago was a significant change, and your belief in my dreams has been the wind in my sails.

I extend my gratitude to my colleagues, mentors, and friends who have shared their insights and wisdom, helping me see leadership from new perspectives.

I must extend my deepest gratitude to Michael Urick, whose collaboration made the writing process not only enjoyable but truly enriching. Working alongside you, Michael, has been a joy and extremely educational experience. Thanks for sharing your knowledge and bringing passion to this project. Co-authoring this book with you and bringing our shared vision to life has been an exciting journey.

I would like to thank all the people who created the Pirates of the Caribbean movie series for inspiring the heart and soul of this book with their stories of bravery, resilience, and daring leadership. Their stories remind us that true leadership is about embracing the unknown with courage and creativity.

A special thanks to the Emerald team, Lydia Cutmore, Daniel Ridge, and especially our editor Fiona Allison for their support and dedication throughout the publication process.

Lastly, to the readers, thank you for embarking on this journey with us. I hope these leadership lessons inspire you to chart your own course and lead with the same adventurous spirit as the legendary pirates of the Caribbean.

—Kohn

I would first like to thank my family, especially Lucy, Janet, and my parents Mickie and Rick. Each of you has been so supportive in the process of not just writing this book but all of the books that I have written over the years. Thank you. And thank you, each of you, for watching various movies in the "Pirates of the Caribbean" series with me. Especially, thanks to my parents for introducing me to the original "Pirates of the Caribbean" ride during our trips to Disney World when I was a kid and for watching the first film in the series with me while we were on vacation at the beach 20 years ago.

I would also like to thank Lana Dillon, who works as an assistant to me at Saint Vincent College. I appreciate our conversations and your help in managing my schedule so that I can squeeze in working on fun passion projects such as this book.

I, of course, want to thank my co-author, Dr. Pelin Kohn, who made working on this book enjoyable and almost effortless. I enjoyed learning from you and engaging in the process of putting this book together with you.

Walt Disney was the original creative mind behind the "Pirates of the Caribbean" ride and I thank you and your team of Imagineers who worked on this attraction that sparked my imagination and the imagination of countless other visitors to the Disney parks. I should also thank the creative teams, including the writers, directors, producers, actors, and others that worked on the "Pirates of the Caribbean" film series and brought these memorable characters to life.

The exceptional team at Emerald must be thanked. Lydia Cutmore, Daniel Ridge, and especially Fiona Allison, the best Books Commissioning Editor in the world!

Lastly, thank you, the readers! We hope that you enjoy this book and might even take away a few nuggets of inspiration to help you on your leadership journey.

—Urick

1

INTRODUCTION

CHARTING THE COURSE OF LEADERSHIP THROUGH THE HIGH SEAS

The concept of effective leadership has changed dramatically in the 21st century due to technological advancements, cultural diversity, and economic shifts. In the same way, pirate captains in "Pirates of the Caribbean" navigated dangerous seas, today's leaders, must have the ability to guide their organizations through these complexities with competence and vision. Modern leadership challenges can be compared to the high-stakes world of piracy to gain profound insights into the qualities that define effective leadership today.

Today's leaders are expected to possess a dynamic skill set that enables them to navigate through these complexities with competence and vision. Hence, effective leadership characteristics are constantly evolving, and continuous learning is critical to enhancing leadership capabilities in the modern era.

CHARACTERISTICS OF EFFECTIVE LEADERSHIP

Effective leadership in the contemporary world requires adaptability and flexibility. In response to changing market conditions, technological innovations, and global trends, leaders must be agile. Much like the legendary Captain Jack Sparrow from "Pirates of the Caribbean," who navigates treacherous seas and unpredictable allies with an intelligent mind, modern leaders must be agile. This adaptability allows them to steer their organizations through shifting market conditions, technological innovations, and global trends with confidence.

Just as Jack Sparrow leverages every tool at his disposal to outwit his enemies, contemporary leaders must be technologically savvy. Leaders need to stay informed about new developments and understand how to leverage these technologies to improve organizational efficiency, productivity, and communication.

Modern leadership also requires emotional intelligence (EI) similar to how Sparrow reads and influences the emotions of his crew to maintain loyalty and morale. Those with high EI are adept at managing their own emotions and understand and influence the emotions of others within their organizations. This skill is invaluable for building strong teams, resolving conflicts, and maintaining high levels of employee engagement and morale.

In today's organizations, cultural competence is more important than ever because of the globalized business environment. Just as the crew of the Black Pearl comprises a diverse group with varied backgrounds, effective leaders must navigate cultural differences to create an inclusive environment where all team members can thrive. By embracing diversity, leaders can harness the unique strengths of each individual, much like Sparrow does with his eclectic crew.

Visionary thinking is essential for leaders who need to look beyond daily operations and envision what their organizations can achieve in the future. Like Jack Sparrow's unyielding pursuit of the horizon, visionary leaders think innovatively and strategically, guiding their organizations toward long-term success despite the uncertainties ahead.

Integrity and ethical leadership are the foundation of trust within and outside of an organization. As Sparrow sometimes faces moral dilemmas, leaders must model ethical behavior and decision-making, establishing a standard that builds trust among stakeholders and ensures the organization's reputation remains intact.

Collaborative skills are crucial as organizational structures become less hierarchical and more project-based. Just as Captain Sparrow must collaborate with others, even rivals, to achieve his goals, effective leaders need to work across boundaries, fostering team cohesion and cooperation. By being continuous learners and embracing collaboration, leaders can ensure their teams work together smoothly to achieve common objectives, no matter how challenging the journey may be.

Effective leaders must be able to collaborate across boundaries by being continuous learners and ensure team cohesion and cooperation to achieve common goals.

THE IMPORTANCE OF CONTINUOUS LEARNING IN LEADERSHIP

Leadership requires continuous learning to keep up with the fast-changing business landscape. As a result, leaders should remain up-to-date with new trends, technologies, and methodologies, enabling them to make more informed decisions and to address complex problems strategically.

The continuous learning process also enables leaders to gain a deeper understanding of diverse ideas and experiences, which can lead to creative solutions and encourage a culture of innovation.

Another benefit of ongoing learning is confidence. In addition to learning new skills, leaders refine their existing ones, which leads to improved leadership effectiveness.

Leaders who promote a culture of professional and personal development within their organizations also set a positive example for their teams. This modeling behavior encourages employees to pursue their own learning, leading to a more knowledgeable and versatile workforce.

Additionally, as the workforce becomes more diverse, understanding generational shifts is essential. Continuous learning helps leaders grasp the values, communication styles, and work preferences of different generations, enhancing team dynamics and effectiveness.

In a global and technologically advanced market, effective leadership requires a blend of traditional and new-age skills. Continuous learning stands out as a fundamental element for leaders aiming to enhance their skills and lead their organizations successfully. Leadership is not only about keeping up with change but also about thriving, enabling organizations to innovate, adapt, and succeed in the long run. Leaders can learn new skills from various resources and movies are one of them.

But how can leaders learn? The "Exploring Effective Leadership Practices through Popular Culture" book series (Edited by Mike Urick and of which this book is a part) suggests that leaders can learn from just about anything – including fictional movies such as "Pirates of the Caribbean" (POTC). Thus, using the tumultuous and thrilling adventures of the "Pirates of the Caribbean" movie series, this book aims to impart lessons to its readers. With its unique view of leadership dynamics under extreme conditions, this book and series not only entertain but hopefully also suggest profound insights into leadership resilience, adaptability, and the nuance of human traits and behaviors in commanding positions.

From the depicted narratives and character dynamics of the "Pirates of the Caribbean," this book offers valuable lessons for modern leadership. Piracy's unpredictable, high-stakes world in the films serves as a powerful metaphor for the complexities and challenges faced by today's leaders.

Like pirate captains in movies, today's leaders must manage uncertainty effectively. Modern leadership environments, such as rapid market dynamics, technological advancements, and cultural shifts, symbolize uncharted waters. Leaders must be able to adapt quickly and effectively to these changes to ensure their organizations remain competitive and resilient.

Characters such as Hector Barbossa demonstrate the importance of strategic flexibility in leadership. As his relationship evolved from foe to ally, he illustrates the need for leaders to consider new alliances and emerging threats when planning tactics and strategies. Leaders must navigate complex situations with foresight and agility, making far-reaching and impactful decisions.

Elizabeth Swann's transformation from a passive to a proactive character illustrates the transformative power of leadership. Her journey illustrates how leadership skills can emerge from within, reshaping one's identity and influencing others in powerful ways. It also highlights the empowerment that comes with embracing leadership roles, especially in communities or fields where representation has traditionally been limited, such as those involving underrepresented groups.

As exemplified by Will Turner's moral dilemmas, ethical integrity is a recurring theme in the series. Leaders often have to make tough decisions that test their values. By reinforcing that ethical leadership is crucial to securing trust and respect, both of which are foundational to effective leadership, the POTC series highlights the importance of maintaining a moral compass.

As a leader, Jack Sparrow epitomizes ingenuity and resourcefulness. His character teaches the value of unconventional thinking and creative problem-solving through his ability to navigate out of seemingly impossible situations. It is important for leaders to learn from Sparrow's approach to leverage their unique strengths and adapt their strategies in order to meet and overcome challenges.

Leadership actions and decisions can be significantly influenced by an understanding and integration of personal and collective histories, as shown in the motivations behind the characters' quests.

Different leadership styles are depicted in the films to explore the nuances of power and authority. There are several complexities involved in wielding authority to command loyalty and respect while also managing fear and admiration dynamics.

EI is demonstrated by the characters, particularly in their interactions and relationships aboard the pirate ships. Leadership requires the ability to understand and manage not only one's own feelings but also those of team members to maintain harmony and influence.

From these leadership themes, this book draws lessons from the high seas that can be applied to contemporary leadership challenges. Whether navigating a political landscape, spearheading innovative projects, or leading a corporate team through economic turbulence, the principles distilled from the cinematic pirate adventures provide a robust framework for effective leadership. Through this book, current and aspiring leaders can cultivate resilience, strategic thinking, ethical judgment, and innovative problem-solving skills, inspiring them to lead with courage, intelligence, and adventure.

As we have explored the foundational leadership qualities, it is time to look at leadership through the lens of popular culture. An in-depth examination of the adventurous and unconventional leadership practices employed by the characters of "Pirates of the Caribbean" is provided in Chapter 2, "The Captain's Code Leadership Strategies from The Caribbean."

2

THE CAPTAIN'S CODE

LEADERSHIP STRATEGIES FROM THE CARIBBEAN

Every leader has their own style of leading others, making decisions, dealing with change, influencing others, and accomplishing personal and organizational goals. Leadership theories explain the processes, traits, behaviors, and contexts that contribute to effective leadership by identifying the differences between leaders. The theories provide frameworks for understanding how leaders influence others, make decisions, and achieve organizational objectives (Kets de Vries & Cheak, 2015). These theories explore various aspects of leadership to identify what makes a leader effective (Penney et al., 2015), how leaders develop, and how leadership can be improved. Throughout this book, leadership theories, such as trait, behavioral, transformational, transactional, servant, and ethical, will be used to analyze the leaders in the "Pirates of the Caribbean" series.

THEORIES OF LEADERSHIP IN A NUTSHELL

Transformational Leadership Theory

Transformational leaders inspire and elevate those around them by creating a compelling vision for the future. This type of leadership is characterized by four key components: intellectual stimulation, individualized consideration, and idealized influence.

Intellectual stimulation implies encouraging innovation and creativity within an organization. Transformational leaders challenge their team members to think critically and solve problems in new ways. In order to ensure continuous growth and learning, they foster an environment where assumptions are questioned and new possibilities are explored.

Individualized consideration refers to the leader's ability to attend to each follower's unique needs and aspirations. Transformational leaders act as mentors, offering personalized support and encouragement. Team leaders help their team members reach their full potential by understanding their strengths, weaknesses, and motivations.

Idealized influence is the degree to which leaders serve as role models for their followers. Transformational leaders demonstrate high standards of ethical behavior and integrity, earning the respect and trust of those they lead. Through their actions, they inspire others to emulate their commitment and values, thus fostering an organization-wide culture of excellence.

Situational Leadership Theories

According to situational leadership theories, leaders must adapt their leadership style depending on the maturity and competence of their followers and the demands of the situation. To provide the appropriate direction and support, these theories emphasize the importance of flexibility and the ability to diagnose followers' needs.

Servant Leadership Theory

According to servant leadership theory, leaders prioritize their followers and the organization's needs over their own. The theory focuses on empathy, listening, stewardship, and the development and well-being of followers.

Authentic Leadership Theory

In authentic leadership theory, leaders are emphasized as being genuine, transparent, and true to their values. When leaders consistently align their actions with their beliefs and values, they build trust and credibility with their followers.

Transactional Leadership Theory

A transactional leadership approach consists of clear structures and expectations, which reward compliance and punish deviations. Maintaining efficiency and meeting performance standards is the primary objective.

Relational Leadership Theory

Relational leadership focuses on developing strong, trust-based connections and fostering a collaborative, inclusive environment. Leaders prioritize empowering followers, promoting ethical behavior, and making decisions collaboratively.

It's unlikely many would have thought that a fictional story about pirates roaming the high seas in the mid-1700s would have such relevance to the present industrial infrastructure globally. But in fact, the "Pirates of the Caribbean" series provides a useful and interesting framework for thinking ahead and making business-related decisions in the 21st century. Let's examine the theories explained above on how to lead like a pirate, and we'll tie it all together with the swashbuckling crew of Pirates of the Caribbean (Verbinski, 2003).

CAPTAIN JACK SPARROW: TRANSFORMATIONAL LEADERSHIP

Leadership includes intelligence, self-confidence, and charisma. And if there's one pirate captain who fits the bill, it's Captain Jack Sparrow. He's got that certain *je ne sais quoi* that sets him apart from the rest of the crew.

Jack's leadership style is all about charm, wit, and a bit of daring. He's not afraid to take risks, and he's always got a clever plan up his sleeve. People are naturally drawn to him, whether it's because of his roguish good looks, his quick tongue, or his devil-may-care attitude. When Jack speaks, people listen, and they're eager to follow him wherever he goes.

While Jack might not be the most academically gifted pirate on the Seven Seas, he's certainly not lacking in the self-confidence department. His charisma is off the charts. Just watch the way he talks his way out of tight spots or the way he's always got a quip at the ready.

Jack's natural charm, quick wit, and daring spirit make him a true leader. His resourcefulness and adaptability ensure that he's always one step ahead of the competition. Jack's confidence and charisma are infectious. He's able to inspire his crew to do things they never thought possible, whether it's taking on the might of the East India Trading Company or diving down to the depths of the ocean to retrieve a chest of cursed gold. His quick wit and silver tongue have saved the day more times than anyone can count.

But it's not just Jack's natural qualities that make him a great leader. He's also incredibly resourceful and adaptable. He's able to think on his feet and come up with a plan, no matter how dire the situation is. He's not afraid to get his hands dirty, and he's always willing to put himself in harm's way to protect his crew. Despite his roguish exterior, he's got a heart of gold, and he genuinely cares about the people he's leading.

Through his remarkable ability to inspire a shared vision, Captain Jack Sparrow, the legendary pirate captain known for his flamboyant style and audacious exploits, exemplifies transformational leadership. Often ambitious and filled with adventure, Sparrow's grand visions capture the attention of his crew and allies. Even though his unconventional methods often appear chaotic, he ignites a sense of excitement and possibility in those who follow him. In Sparrow's infectious enthusiasm and daring spirit, his crew is encouraged to embark on perilous quests, uniting them for a common goal. In fostering this shared vision, he transforms a divided group into a motivated and cohesive team, willing to take risks and overcome obstacles.

Captain Jack Sparrow's transformational leadership also includes individualized consideration. Sparrow is well-aware of his crew members' unique strengths and weaknesses. His leadership approach is tailored to meet the specific needs and talents of each individual. He recognizes Mr. Gibbs' loyalty and navigational skills, often relying on him for crucial decisions. Also, he acknowledges Will Turner's swordsmanship and bravery, assigning him challenging tasks that match his abilities.

As a result, Sparrow empowers his crew to excel in their respective roles, enhancing their overall performance and satisfaction. Personalized attention not only boosts morale but also fosters loyalty and respect toward Sparrow. As a result of his ability to see and nurture each crew member's potential, everyone feels valued and motivated to perform at their best. In this way, Sparrow cultivates a supportive and dynamic team capable of achieving extraordinary feats.

Captain Jack Sparrow's transformational leadership is characterized by his ability to inspire a shared vision and his commitment to individual consideration. In the first "Pirates of the Caribbean" movie, "The Curse of the Black Pearl," Jack inspires his crew by talking about reclaiming the Black Pearl, a ship that symbolizes freedom and the pirate life. He convinces the crew that they would have the fastest ship in the Caribbean if they controlled the Black Pearl, as well as the freedom to follow their own desires and dreams without limitations. This vision motivates his crew to take risks and follow him despite the dangers ahead, as they see the potential rewards of their shared goal.

His ability to unite his crew around bold, adventurous goals, combined with his attention to their individual needs, makes him an effective leader. As a transformational leader, Sparrow promotes a sense of camaraderie and growth among his crew while driving them toward success.

CAPTAIN HECTOR BARBOSSA:
TRANSFORMATIONAL LEADERSHIP

Depending on the situation, leaders must use different leadership strategies (Moniz, 2010) to motivate others. Captain Barbossa demonstrates transformational leadership by not only guiding his crew through dangerous situations but also motivating them to reach great achievements.

Hector Barbossa is an example of a transformational leader due to his emphasis on intellectual stimulation. In addition to challenging his crew to think critically and creatively, he pushes them to explore new ideas and approaches outside of their comfort zones. Barbossa promotes an environment where innovative solutions and questions of assumptions are encouraged. Crew members gain ingenuity and resourcefulness as a result of this culture of intellectual growth and exploration. Barbossa ensures his crew remains adaptive and forward-thinking by promoting intellectual stimulation, thereby enabling them to navigate the unpredictable world of piracy confidently and effectively. In "Pirates of the Caribbean: On Stranger Tides," when Barbossa becomes a privateer for the British Crown, he transforms from a pirate captain to a naval officer, pushing his crew to adapt to this new, more structured environment. To balance their pirate instincts with the discipline of the navy, the crew must think creatively. By encouraging his men to navigate this dual identity and come up with innovative solutions to the challenges that come with serving two masters, Barbossa fosters intellectual stimulation.

Barbossa's transformational leadership can also be seen in his idealized influence. Leading by example, he embodies the pirate code and adheres to his principles without wavering (Marshall, 2011; Nawaz & Khan, 2016). Through his actions and decisions, he consistently demonstrates the values he holds dear, earning his crew's respect and loyalty. Barbossa inspires the people around him with his integrity and steadfastness. His crew members look up to him not only as a leader but also as a role model. Using his idealized influence, Barbossa cultivates a loyal and motivated team driven by shared values and goals.

As a transformational leader, Captain Hector Barbossa emphasizes intellectual stimulation and idealized influence. A compelling leader, he challenges and inspires his crew to think creatively while adhering steadfastly to his principles. Creating a culture of intellectual growth and leading by example, Barbossa builds a team capable of achieving extraordinary feats.

Barbossa is always one step ahead of the game. He's able to anticipate potential problems and come up with a plan of action before anyone else even knows what's going on. He's not afraid to switch things up when the situation calls for it, whether it's negotiating with other pirates or fighting off the Navy. He's always willing to adapt his leadership style to suit the needs of his crew and the situation at hand.

WILL TURNER: SERVANT LEADERSHIP

Will Turner embodies servant leadership through his unwavering commitment to others. We see that building strong relationships between leaders and their followers is essential to good leadership. And who better to personify that than Will Turner, the blacksmith turned pirate?

As he continues his journey, Turner consistently puts the needs of his crew and loved ones before his own desires. To ensure the safety and success of those under his leadership, he accepts significant responsibilities and risks with a deep sense of duty and selflessness. His dedication to serving others is evident in the many sacrifices he makes, including putting himself in harm's way to protect and support his crew. A perfect example of Will

Turner's selflessness and dedication to others is the moment he stabs the heart of Davy Jones and becomes the Captain of the Flying Dutchman. Will saves not only his loved ones but also the rest of his crew, ensuring their survival. This act requires him to sacrifice his own desires and future, as he is bound to the Flying Dutchman and its eternal duty of carrying souls. Despite the personal cost, Will's willingness to take on this immense responsibility exemplifies his commitment to serving others and exemplifies the leadership qualities of duty and selflessness. His selflessness earns him the respect and loyalty of his followers as well as creating a strong sense of trust and camaraderie within the team. Turner fosters a supportive and cohesive environment where everyone feels cared for and motivated to work together by placing the well-being of others at the forefront of his leadership approach.

Another key aspect of Will Turner's servant leadership is his commitment to empowering others. Will consistently supports Elizabeth in her growth from the governor's daughter into a strong, independent leader and pirate. Even when it means going against societal norms, he trusts her abilities, respects her decisions, and stands by her side. When Elizabeth decides to take on the role of Pirate King, Will not only supports her but also encourages her leadership in the battle against Lord Beckett's fleet. His belief in Elizabeth's abilities allows her to step into her power and become a key figure in the struggle for freedom.

As a leader, Turner understands the importance of delegation and trusts his crew to carry out important tasks. By doing so, he creates an environment where everyone feels valued and capable of contributing to the team's goals. Turner's leadership style encourages autonomy and personal growth, as he provides his crew with the opportunities and support they need to develop their skills and confidence. The empowerment of crew members enhances the overall effectiveness of the team and fosters pride and ownership among them. His willingness to entrust his followers with critical responsibilities demonstrates Turner's servant leadership philosophy, whose primary objective is to serve and uplift others.

Will Turner's servant leadership is characterized by his selfless dedication to empowering his crew. As a result of his actions, his team is more supportive and trusting, which demonstrates a deep sense of responsibility and care. In "Pirates of the Caribbean: At World's End," when Will agrees to a risky plan to rescue Jack Sparrow from Davy Jones' Locker, the crew of the Black Pearl, including key figures like Elizabeth Swann and Captain

Barbossa, support him without hesitation. In spite of the dangers and uncertainties, they follow Will's lead because they trust his judgment and believe in his commitment. In addition to ensuring his crew's success, Turner cultivates a culture of mutual respect and collaboration by valuing and empowering them. In his servant leadership approach, he emphasizes the importance of prioritizing the needs of others and creating an environment where everyone can thrive and contribute to the team's success.

Will might not be the flashiest member of the crew, but he's always looking out for his friends and crew. He's the one who's willing to put himself in harm's way to protect others, whether it's rescuing Jack Sparrow from the clutches of Davy Jones or facing down the Kraken to save his friends. But it's not just Will's bravery that makes him a great leader. It's his ability to connect with others on a deep and personal level. He's not afraid to show vulnerability, and he's always willing to listen to others and offer a shoulder to cry on. Whether it's mentoring a young sailor or offering words of comfort to a grieving friend, Will knows that building strong relationships is key to being a good leader.

ELIZABETH SWANN: SITUATIONAL LEADERSHIP

As a situational leader, Elizabeth Swann demonstrates the ability to adapt her leadership style to a variety of situations. This theory suggests that the best leaders are the ones who can adapt their leadership style to suit the situation and the people they're leading. And none can better exemplify it than Elizabeth Swann, the governor's daughter turned pirate captain.

Elizabeth starts off as a prim and proper young lady, but she quickly learns to adapt to the rough-and-tumble world of piracy. She's able to change her leadership style to fit the needs of her crew and the situations they find themselves in. Whether she's negotiating with other pirates, fighting off the Navy, or leading her crew into battle, she's always able to find the right approach to get the job done.

A leader of exceptional versatility, Swan seamlessly transitions between various approaches to achieve the best results. Swann builds alliances and navigates complex political landscapes using her diplomatic and strategic skills when dealing with other leaders. Through her diplomatic approach, she is capable of effectively managing conflicts, fostering cooperation, and securing advantageous positions for her crew.

Swann can also be assertive and decisive when circumstances require immediate action. In dangerous or high-stakes situations, she confidently takes charge, making swift and informed decisions to ensure the crew's safety and success. During critical moments, her assertiveness inspires confidence and trust among her followers, who trust her guidance to navigate perilous challenges. As a result of Swann's ability to adjust her leadership style according to situational demands, her actions are always aligned with the current context and requirements.

Situational leadership requires Elizabeth Swann to carefully evaluate her crew members' readiness and capabilities (Thompson & Glasø, 2015). Every member of Swann's team is given the time and attention they deserve based on their skills, experience, and developmental needs. In "At World's End," Elizabeth demonstrates individualized consideration when she becomes the Pirate King. She shows an understanding of the unique skills and strengths of her crew members, such as Will Turner, a skilled swordsman and strategist, and Captain Sao Feng, a seasoned pirate with considerable influence in the pirate world. Elizabeth leverages the strengths of each person to orchestrate a plan that will ultimately lead to the success of their mission to defeat the East India Trading Company and free Jack Sparrow.

As a result, she can assign crew members tasks that match their strengths, ensuring their success. She can delegate responsibilities effectively because she understands her team's abilities, maximizing their performance and efficiency. Elizabeth is also a great listener. She's not afraid to take advice from her crew, and she's always willing to consider their opinions when making decisions. Elizabeth, as the newly elected Pirate King, must decide on the course of action for the pirates in their fight against the East India Trading Company. Even though she is in a position of authority, Elizabeth listens carefully to the advice of her fellow pirates, including Captain Jack Sparrow and Captain Hector Barbossa. Before making a final decision, she weighs Jack's unconventional yet insightful strategies with Barbossa's experience and tactical insight.

She knows that her crew is only as strong as its weakest member, so she's always looking out for everyone's best interests. Swann also invests in the growth and development of her crew members. She helps them build their confidence and competence by providing ongoing guidance and support. In Dead Man's Chest, Elizabeth encourages Will to take on more leadership responsibilities. She provides him with support and guidance, helping him navigate dangerous and complex situations. When Will hesitates in making critical decisions or doubts his abilities, Elizabeth steps in to reassure him, offering her perspective and reinforcing his strengths. Through this ongoing support, Will grows into a more capable and confident leader.

Swann fosters an environment where her team can grow and evolve as leaders by providing mentorship and skill development opportunities. She ensures a sustainable leadership pipeline within her team by focusing on readiness assessment and development. Her approach empowers her followers to take on greater responsibilities and contributes to their long-term success.

Elizabeth Swann's situational leadership style is characterized by her flexibility in adapting her leadership style and her commitment to assessing and developing her crew members' readiness. Depending on the situation, she can be both diplomatic and assertive, enabling her to effectively deal with a wide range of challenges. In addition, she nurtures a strong, competent, and motivated crew by understanding and supporting their capabilities. Swann's situational leadership approach emphasizes the importance of adaptability, readiness assessment, and development support.

The Situational Theory reminds us that leadership is not a one-size-fits-all proposition. The best leaders are the ones who are able to adapt to the situation at hand and tailor their approach to fit the needs of their crew.

TIA DALMA: AUTHENTIC LEADERSHIP

Through her unwavering embrace of her true self, Tia Dalma embodies the essence of authentic leadership through her mystical prowess and enigmatic charm. Her unapologetically authentic identity, marked by mystical powers and a unique worldview, sets her apart from other leaders. Authenticity defines her leadership style and sets a powerful example for those around her. Dalma encourages her followers to recognize and embrace their own strengths and identities through authenticity and confidence. As a result, individuals feel empowered to express themselves in a culture of acceptance and self-expression. Therefore, Dalma's leadership inspires others to shed any facades and stand firmly in their own truths.

Dalma possesses an exceptional level of emotional intelligence, which is a key aspect of her authentic leadership. In "Pirates of the Caribbean: Dead Man's Chest" and "At World's End," Tia Dalma shows deep empathy and understanding of Davy Jones's emotional turmoil. Even though Jones appears cruel and hardened, Tia Dalma recognizes the pain and love that still reside within him. The way she speaks to him, it is clear that she understands his suffering and the motives behind his actions. Tia Dalma demonstrates her emotional intelligence by seeing beyond Jones' anger and bitterness to understand the underlying emotions that motivate him.

She also understands the emotions and motivations that drive other people. While Tia Dalma may not lead a crew in the traditional pirate sense, her influence is undeniable. She commands respect and loyalty through her wisdom, emotional intelligence, and ability to read and control others' emotions and motivations. With this insight, she is able to reach out to them deeply on a personal level, fostering trust and camaraderie that are essential to their success. Dalma's innate ability to empathize and relate to her followers' feelings helps her create an environment in which they feel valued and understood. It is this connection that not only solidifies their loyalty to her but also makes them more willing to follow her lead with dedication. Using her emotional intelligence, Dalma builds a cohesive, resilient team capable of navigating challenges together. Therefore, her leadership is characterized by a strong relational foundation, underpinned by mutual respect and genuine care.

Tia Dalma exemplifies authentic leadership in an inspiring and effective way by embodying these principles. Her deep emotional intelligence and embrace of her true self-serve as critical pillars of her leadership, creating an environment of acceptance, trust, and personal connection.

DAVY JONES: TRANSACTIONAL LEADERSHIP

Transactional is all about efficiency and organization and who better to demonstrate this characteristic than Davy Jones himself? Jones might be a bit of a tyrant, but there's no denying that his ship, the Flying Dutchman, runs like a well-oiled machine. He's got his crew working in perfect synchronization, and he's always got a plan for how to get what he wants.

Jones is a master at delegating tasks to his crew, and he knows exactly how to motivate them to work hard and stay focused. He's not afraid to crack the whip, when necessary, but he also knows how to reward his crew for a job well done. Whether it's a bonus for capturing a particularly elusive soul or a chance to indulge in a favorite pastime, Jones knows how to keep his crew happy and productive.

MR. GIBBS: RELATIONAL LEADERSHIP

Continuing our journey through the world of pirate leadership, we enter the domain of Relational Theory, which looks at what leaders actually do rather than their innate traits or abilities. And if there's one pirate who's got behavior down to a science, it's Mr. Gibbs.

Gibbs might not be the flashiest member of the crew, but he's always doing the grunt work that keeps the ship running smoothly. Whether it's swabbing the deck or patching up the ship, he's always ready to roll up his sleeves and get his hands dirty. But it's not just his work ethic that makes him a great leader – it's his compassion and empathy (Popper, 2004; Underdal, 1994).

Gibbs is always there to offer a sympathetic ear or a word of advice to anyone who needs it. He's the glue that holds the crew together, and he's always looking out for the best interests of his fellow pirates (Akpoviroro et al., 2018). Whether it's counseling Jack Sparrow on matters of the heart or helping Will Turner through a difficult time, Gibbs is always ready to lend a helping hand.

We see that collaboration and teamwork are essential to good leadership. A trait perfectly embodied by the entire crew of the Black Pearl? Whether they're facing the East India Trading Company or just trying to divide up a haul of treasure, they always work together to achieve their goals.

Each member of the crew has their own unique skills and strengths, and they're always willing to listen to each other and find a compromise. They might not always agree on the best course of action, but they know that by working together, they can achieve anything they set their minds to.

Whether it's Jack Sparrow's daring schemes, Barbossa's strategic thinking, or Elizabeth Swann's adaptability, the crew of the Black Pearl knows that they're stronger together than they are apart. They're not just a group of pirates; they're a family bound together by loyalty, respect, and a shared sense of adventure.

So, there you have it – the leadership theories as embodied by pirates from The Pirates of the Caribbean. Whether it's running a tight ship or building strong relationships, these pirates know that good leadership is all about balancing efficiency with compassion and always striving to be the best they can be.

SUMMARY

This chapter explored different leadership theories that identify leaders' decision-making, influence on others, and success in achieving personal and organizational objectives. Specifically, we considered the following:

- Transformational leaders inspire and motivate followers to achieve extraordinary results while creating a compelling vision and serving as role models.

- Situational leaders provide appropriate direction and support, demonstrating flexibility and problem-solving ability. They adjust their leadership style based on the maturity and competence of their followers, as well as the demands of the situation.

- Servant leaders prioritize followers' and organizational needs over personal gains. Their leadership focuses on empathy, listening, stewardship, and follower development. They also empower others by delegating tasks and trusting them to make critical decisions.

- Empathic leaders emphasize being genuine, transparent, and true to personal values. They also build trust and credibility by consistently aligning actions with beliefs, which results from demonstrating high emotional intelligence to deeply connect with followers.

- Transactional leaders focus on maintaining order, compliance, and efficiency through a system of rewards and punishments.

- Relational leaders emphasize building strong, collaborative relationships and fostering an inclusive and empowering environment.

After exploring the mechanics of leadership theories, let's explore the heart of effective leadership. Our next chapter will explore how trust can create thriving relationships, transforming leadership into more than just a strategy.

3

BUILDING TRUST AMONG A CREW

Trust seems to be in short supply, both in modern real-world organizations and among the crews of fictional pirates in the "Pirates of the Caribbean" series. In the latter, we see scenes of characters (including Captain Jack Sparrow, Will Turner, and former Commodore James Norrington in a memorable exchange where they vie for Davy Jones' treasure chest or in a scene where multiple characters each point pistols with each other because no one trusts anyone else) switch dueling partners regular. It's hard to trust other when you're constantly dueling them. The characters in "Pirates of the Caribbean" seem to constantly be sparring with each other in one second despite appearing to be friends a few seconds prior. The reason for this is, of course, that these characters do not trust each other.

This phenomenon does not just occur among these "Pirates of the Caribbean" crews. It also occurs in the businesses, nonprofits, agencies, and groups in which we work. In our own organizations, we see a lack of trust when there is gossiping, incivility, and breakdowns in processes due to lack of communication.

Yet, some crews, both pirates and in our own organizations, do stick together to accomplish goals. Work gets done and crews contribute to an agreed upon outcome. But, only those crews that have trust will be able to accomplish their goals. Thus, leaders need to build trust in order to get their crew to accomplish a goal.

TYPES OF TRUST

Trust can be defined a number of different ways. One way is that trust is a reliance or dependence on someone (Merriam-Webster, n.d.). Many organizational scholars have suggested that there are at least three types of trust (Baer & Colquitt, 2018): disposition-based, cognitive-based, and affect-based.

Disposition-based trust has more to do with the truster than the potential trustee. In other words, it is related to the propensity that each individual is predisposed to regarding how much they generally trust others. This has a lot to do with their personality. While no one in the "Pirates of the Caribbean" series is perhaps too inclined to trust others, Elizabeth Swann comes the closest in the first film "Curse of the Black Pearl." When she is captured by pirates, she trusts them in part to keep their word about the practice of "parley." She also shows trust in eating, even if somewhat reluctantly, the food provided by Captain Hector Barbossa during one of their first meetings despite the fact that it might be poisoned.

Perhaps more apparent in "Pirates of the Caribbean" is cognitive-based trust. Cognitive-based trust concerns thinking about whether someone can trust another. Thoughts of the truster can be based on perceptions of benevolence, a person's track record, their skills, or other attributes. In "Pirates of the Caribbean," Will Turner trusts Captain Jack Sparrow to help him find Elizabeth Swann. He, at least at first, does not have much affection for Jack Sparrow but seeks his aid because of his experiences of being a pirate. In other words, Will cognitively understands that Jack Sparrow may be able to help him based on his background in piracy.

Affect-based trust comes with time. This type of trust is about an emotional connection that the truster has with the trustee. It is rarer than the other types because it develops through extensive experience with the person. Captain Jack Sparrow seems to develop this type of trust among followers. Early on in the series, Captain Jack seems to be disliked by many characters based on the way that they talk about and interact with him. But, as time goes on, he begins to be viewed by other characters (and the audience) as endearing. So much so that, when he disappears for a time after being swallowed by the Kraken, others experience regret at his missing. This emotional connection did not occur immediately – it took time for the characters and audiences to warm up to Jack Sparrow. Along with this liking, others have come to trust him in some manner because of having a positive emotional connection to him.

In "The Curse of the Black Pearl," Captain Jack Sparrow remarks that he is dishonest. And because of that, he suggests that he should be trusted because he will always be this way. This paradox is interesting. While Sparrow seems to joke that he is untrustworthy, there is some logic to his statement. As such, Sparrow builds cognitive-based trust by logically explaining what others can expect of him. Couple this with his affect-based trust that he earns due to his likeability factor, it is not surprising that he is able to lead and influence others based on trust.

Davy Jones also sees a surprising level of commitment from his crew, an outcome of trust. But, why is this the case given his devious nature? Why does his crew stay – is it because they are forced via a transactional type of leadership (Avolio et al., 1999) whereby they would be punished if they were to leave. Or is there more there to this the trust that Jones finds among his crew? Actually, it may be that the crew cognitively trusts Davy Jones – despite being someone who physically punishes his crew and captures souls to serve him, he does actually get results in taking over the seas. Therefore, the crew might believe in his ability to help them get the results that they desire.

Davy Jones' crew might also experience affect-based trust among each other due to having lived through the experience of serving on Jones' ship The Flying Dutchman and building an emotional bond that way. The crew, especially Boot Strap Bill, like to say that they are part of the group and part of the ship regularly. Thus, they might follow Davy Jones not so much because they trust him but because the members have built a camaraderie among each other based on trust. Thus, they all work together well and trust each other to accomplish their goals. Jones just happens to be the captain of that particular team that trusts each other.

IMPORTANCE OF TRUST

By building trust, leaders will see many positive outcomes (Bhattacharya et al., 1998). Some of these include increased commitment, lower turnover, and higher team performance. Of course, if we are to understand how best we can build trust among our own crews, we must understand some additional areas of group dynamics including the stages of team development and how it relates to trust. As a reminder, the crew can trust the leader, but performance may increase when the team members also trust themselves as in the case with Davy Jones.

According to classic research by Tuckman (1965), there are five stages to team development: forming, storming, norming, performing, and adjourning.

Those teams that are the furthest along with regard to their team stage are most likely to possess the strongest trust. In other words, trust is built through the process of going through these stages as a crew because the stages build a common way of thinking through shared experiences. Along with this comes a sense of trust.

The first stage is forming. This is when a crew gets together for the first time. The members likely do not know each other, they don't trust each other, and they might not even know the purpose of the team or why they are a part of it. There is a lot of uncertainty in this stage. In the "Pirates of the Caribbean" series, a crew is put together in the film "At World's End" to attempt to convene the Brethren Court by getting the Nine Pirate Lords together. The crew that is being put together is comprised of a variety of sailors who have served under different captains in the past as well as many who have been captains themselves. Many of them have not worked together in the past by serving on the same crew and it is unclear to them why (or how) they have to assist Jack Sparrow who is one of the Pirate Lords.

The second stage is storming. In this stage, there is a lot of conflict, disagreement, and misunderstanding. While this happens throughout the quest to find Jack Sparrow in "At World's End," it is most apparent when the Brethren Court finally assembles on Shipwreck Cove. It is in this meeting where the crew comprised by a many smaller crews of pirates must elect a Pirate King to lead them all in their quest to rid the seas of Davy Jones and the East India Trading Company. There is much disagreement on how to defeat Davy Jones and the East India Trading Company and especially who should be chosen as the Pirate King. It seems that each leader of their respective crew wants to be elected as Pirate King.

The third stage is norming. In this stage, teams decide on their roles and start to work together. In "At World's End," the pirate crews unite around Elizabeth Swann as the Pirate King and come up with a plan on how to invoke the goddess Calypso to help aid their fight against Davy Jones. She is elected by one vote and, though initially each pirate captain wanted themselves to be the Pirate King, they ultimately come to accept Elizabeth in her leadership role and launch their ships in order to play their parts in bringing down Davy Jones.

The fourth stage is performing. Together, the Pirate Lords work together to release Calypso which aids in defeating Davy Jones. Ultimately, the pirates accomplish their goal of being able to sail free again. Davy Jones is defeated and the East India Company seems to have been hurt badly enough to leave the pirates alone to be free to sail the seas.

The final stage is adjourning. In this stage, the team goes their separate ways. Of course, every crew breaks up at some point including those in "Pirates of the Caribbean." In "At World's End," Will Turner assumes command of The Flying Dutchman, Elizabeth Swann seemingly relinquishes her post as Pirate King, and each of the separate pirate crews are assumed to go about their own business and not stay with the larger combined crew.

It should be noted that, throughout this process of team development, camaraderie is built. Along with camaraderie comes trust. Thus, there are some characteristics of teams that help to develop trust over time. When developing a crew, there are some things (Morgeson et al., 2005) that captains should consider. For example, each individual's skills, each person's experience on teams, and the size of teams are things to consider. Perhaps most importantly, is that teams that go through common experiences together form shared mental models which are ways of thinking that each member possesses. Typically, those crews that make it to the norming and performing stages have developed these ways of thinking and, in doing so, have developed trust. While this does not guarantee a higher performance, it is likely that those teams that do reach these levels could have a higher chance of increased performance.

BREAKING TRUST

While trust can come from shared experiences and is related to motivation level and ultimately performance, the opposite is also true. The crew that lacks trust may find itself to be unmotivated and not perform well. Early on in the series, Jack Sparrow had seemingly not built up his trust yet among his crew. It seems that they were not receiving the amount of treasure that they had hoped for so cognitive-based trust was likely low because the crew did not believe in Sparrow's competence. Therefore, they mutinied against him and made Hector Barbossa the Captain.

Even if a crew stays after trust with a leader has been lost, they do not function well and may not do so until trust can be rebuilt which could take a considerable amount of time. Even after Jack Sparrow returns from his exile after the mutiny and seeks to become Captain of the Black Pearl again, his former crew does not trust him immediately. Nor do they perform exceptionally well. Ultimately, they are unsuccessful (under the leadership of Barbossa) – though they do break the curse of the Black Pearl, the crew is in disarray and several pirates (seemingly including Barbossa … at least for a time) are killed in the process.

SUMMARY

This chapter explored the importance that trust plays in the functioning of a crew. Specifically, we considered the following:

- There are three types of trust that should be considered when leaders seek to build trust; one type is based on the propensity of followers to trust, another is based on a cognitive evaluation of the trustworthiness of a leader, and the third is based on an emotional connection to the leader.

- Trust is related to increased motivation, commitment, and ultimately performance. Those crews that have common experiences, possess shared mental models, and have progressed through many developmental stages tend to have higher levels of trust among members and toward the leader.

- When trust is not present among a crew, it is likely to experience negative effects, and it may be difficult to rebuild that trust.

Just as building trust among crew members paves the way for unity and strength, tackling racism and inequalities removes barriers to collaboration. In the next chapter, we'll explore how to break down these societal barriers so that everyone can thrive.

4

BREAKING DOWN INEQUALITIES

There are leadership lessons to be learned in the vast expanses of the ocean, where fortunes are born unpredictably and tides of change affect fates. With its swashbuckling adventures and diverse cast of characters, "Pirates of the Caribbean" offers a rich canvas for exploring themes of racism and inequality. Captain Jack Sparrow, Elizabeth Swann, and Hector Barbossa all offer insight into societal injustices through the lens of leadership. Breaking down dysfunctional hierarchies, especially those relating to class and gender, is essential to fostering a more inclusive and equitable society. The characters of Elizabeth Swann and Tia Dalma/Calypso from the "Pirates of the Caribbean" franchise provide excellent examples of how to challenge these norms and build engagement. Their narratives provide insight into challenging traditional gender roles, overcoming objectification, and asserting agency in oppressive environments.

SOCIAL CONSTRUCTION THEORY

Social Construction Theory describes how many aspects of our world, including knowledge, concepts, and categories, are not inherently natural but rather are the result of social processes and interactions. According to this theory, people's perspectives on reality are shaped by the agreements they make and the interactions they have within a society. Our understanding of "truth" and "reality" is mainly a result of social consensus rather than objective reality.

It is important to realize that gender roles and expectations are social constructs rather than inherent or biological. Gender roles are learned behaviors and expectations associated with being male or female, which are influenced by social norms and cultural contexts. Depending on the culture and time period, these roles may differ significantly.

An excellent example of this can be found in the "Pirates of the Caribbean" series. This series tends to portray gender roles as socially constructed rather than natural. Elizabeth Swann is an exemplary example of this concept. Her character journey defies traditional expectations of women by starting out as a proper and respectful lady of her time to becoming a fierce and forceful Pirate King.

Elizabeth evolves into a strong and capable person instead of remaining confined to the passive and domestic roles traditionally assigned to women. Her skills as a swordswoman, a role usually reserved for men, enable her to participate fully in the series' adventures and battles. By changing from a traditional lady to a powerful, independent woman, she illustrates how gender roles can be challenged and redefined. In this progression, we see that gender identity and roles are not innate but are shaped by social influences and are re-shapable through individual choices.

The recognition of gender roles' constructed nature encourages critical thinking about norms and beliefs that are taken for granted, provoking us to question why we believe certain things and to question who our interests serve.

Social Construction Theory provides a valuable lens for understanding how our perceptions of reality are shaped by social processes. In order to work toward more inclusive and equitable societies, we must understand that many aspects of our world, such as gender, race, and knowledge, are constructed through social interactions.

ELIZABETH SWANN: CHALLENGING TRADITIONAL GENDER ROLES

Elizabeth Swann begins the series as a typical upper-class woman, restrained by societal expectations and gender roles. However, as the story progresses, Elizabeth challenges these roles by embracing her strength, resourcefulness, and leadership qualities. Despite being initially portrayed as a helpless woman in need of rescue, Elizabeth soon becomes an active participant in her own story, taking charge of her destiny and engaging with the world around her.

As the "Pirates of the Caribbean" series progresses, Elizabeth becomes a respected pirate captain, illustrating that women are just as capable of leading as men. By assuming this role, Elizabeth disrupts the gender hierarchy that places men above women in leadership positions. Elizabeth consistently defies societal expectations of her gender, taking up sword fighting and engaging in piracy. This defiance creates space for other female characters to break free from traditional roles and assert their autonomy.

TIA DALMA/CALYPSO: OVERCOMING OBJECTIFICATION AND ASSERTING POWER

Tia Dalma/Calypso is a character who embodies power and control despite initially being objectified and restrained by the male characters. Her journey serves as a reminder of the importance of asserting one's agency and subverting the power dynamics inherent in gender and class hierarchies. Tia Dalma/Calypso is ultimately revealed to be a powerful goddess capable of controlling the seas. This transformation serves as a metaphor for women reclaiming their power and autonomy, challenging patriarchal norms.

Throughout the series, Tia Dalma/Calypso is subjected to the male gaze and is often seen as an "exotic" and "mystical" object rather than a person. By asserting her power and reclaiming her true identity, Calypso challenges the objectification of women and the stereotypes associated with her race and gender. Calypso's refusal to be controlled or defined by the male characters in the story demonstrates the importance of asserting one's agency and resisting the constraints imposed by class and gender hierarchies.

DISCUSSION ON GENDER AND GENDER INEQUALITY IN THE CONTEXT OF THE PIRATES OF THE CARIBBEAN SERIES

The "Pirates of the Caribbean" series, while not without its flaws, offers valuable lessons on challenging dysfunctional hierarchies and building engagement. For example, early in the series, we observe a handmaid talking to Elizabeth about marrying a fine young man, implying that it is every woman's wish to do so. Yet, from the start, Elizabeth is not particularly excited by the notion of marriage and being bound to the confines of one home. By examining the journeys of Elizabeth Swann and Tia Dalma/Calypso, we can explore the importance of challenging traditional gender roles, asserting agency and power, and building engagement through representation.

Challenging Traditional Gender Roles

Leaders must recognize the importance of diversity and inclusivity in their teams. An organization benefits from embracing individuals from all backgrounds and skill sets, just as a ship is strengthened by a diverse crew. The motley crew of Captain Jack Sparrow in Pirates of the Caribbean exemplifies this principle. Each member of the team brings unique talents and perspectives, from the resourceful Elizabeth Swann to the enigmatic Tia Dalma. By defying expectations and taking on roles traditionally reserved for men, women can challenge the gender hierarchy and create space for more diverse and equitable representation.

Elizabeth Swann challenges traditional gender roles by rejecting the role of a damsel in distress and actively participating in her own story. She takes charge of her destiny and engages with the world around her. When she becomes a pirate captain, she illustrates that women are just as capable of leading as men. This model reflects gender equality, where individuals have equal rights and opportunities regardless of their gender.

Asserting Agency and Power

Recognizing and asserting one's own power and autonomy is essential for overcoming objectification and challenging the constraints imposed by class and gender hierarchies.

When Elizabeth Swann becomes the Pirate King, she ensures that all pirates have equal representation and a say in the decision-making process, regardless of their gender or background. This model reflects gender equity, where individuals are given equal opportunities and resources to achieve their goals, taking into account their different needs and experiences based on their gender.

In the example of the Black Pearl going head-to-head with the Flying Dutchman in "POTC: At World's End," Elizabeth knows how to take complete advantage of her crew's capabilities. In demonstrating her authority and keen judgment, Elizabeth strategically delegated command of the ship to Captain Barbossa, so he could navigate the rough seas and challenge Davy Jones.

Building Engagement Through Representation

While we acknowledge numerous accomplished female leaders, it's crucial to reflect on the current landscape of women in leadership roles, as evidenced by recent data: approximately 5% of Chief Executive Officer (CEO) positions in Standard & Poor's 500 are held by women (DeFrank-Cole & Tan, 2021).

By including characters like Elizabeth Swann and Tia Dalma/Calypso, the "Pirates of Caribbean" series helps to open up conversations about gender and class inequalities, allowing audiences to engage with these topics and question the hierarchies that perpetuate them. In order to acknowledge gender diversity and actively involve men, the United Nations emphasizes that gender equality encompasses equal rights, responsibilities, and opportunities for men and women (United Nations, Universal declaration of human rights, 1948). In the world of piracy, as in our own, systemic injustices such as racism and inequality lurk beneath the surface, threatening to undermine our society's foundations. Leadership requires us to confront injustice head-on and advocate for change.

The story of Elizabeth Swann's journey from sheltered aristocrat to fierce pirate captain serves as an inspiring example of challenging the status quo. Although Elizabeth faces discrimination and prejudice due to her gender and social status, she refuses to give in to the pressures of society. Rather than letting oppressive systems destroy her, she takes charge of her destiny and fights alongside her crewmates.

Elizabeth Swann's journey in the "Pirates of the Caribbean" series is a valuable example of how gender roles can be challenged, leading to gender equality, equity, and diversity. Elizabeth Swann's journey serves as a reminder of the importance of recognizing the intersectionality of gender with other social identities and how diverse representation and inclusion can challenge traditional gender roles and stereotypes.

One perspective that people often overlook is the impact of colonialism and imperialism on gender relations. POTC is set during the 18th century, a time of great political upheaval, economic transformation, and global expansion. The movie series reflects the imperialist context of the time, where Western powers were engaged in a struggle for dominance and control over non-Western territories and peoples.

Elizabeth's journey as a privileged white woman reflects the gendered power dynamics of the time. The patriarchy and class system that she lives under reinforces the colonialist ideology of Western superiority and non-Western inferiority. However, Elizabeth's journey also reflects the potential for challenging these norms and disrupting the gender hierarchy that reinforces them.

Moreover, Elizabeth's journey intersects with her sexuality, particularly her attraction to Captain Jack Sparrow. As Elizabeth Swann navigates a world dominated by male power structures, her journey highlights the complexities of challenging traditional gender roles. Although she does not directly challenge sexism, she defies gender expectations and asserts herself in traditionally male-dominated spaces, illustrating a broader battle against norms that restrict individual freedom.

Finally, Elizabeth Swann's journey serves as an example of how diverse representation and inclusion can challenge traditional gender roles and stereotypes. The franchise features a diverse cast of characters from different backgrounds, genders, and sexual orientations, which creates space for more inclusive and equitable representations of society. The inclusion of diverse characters also serves as a reminder of the importance of recognizing and challenging the ways in which multiple forms of discrimination intersect and compound each other.

Elizabeth Swann's journey in the "Pirates of the Caribbean" series offers a unique perspective on gender equality, equity, and diversity. By recognizing the intersectionality of gender with other social identities, such as race, class, and sexuality, and promoting diverse representation and inclusion, the franchise challenges traditional gender roles and stereotypes, illustrating the importance of equal rights, opportunities, and treatment of individuals regardless of their gender or social identities. However, it is important to continue to critically examine and address the ways in which multiple forms of discrimination intersect and perpetuate inequality and oppression, particularly in the context of colonialism and imperialism.

EXAMINING THE THEORY OF GENDER AND POWER IN LIGHT OF THE "PIRATES OF THE CARIBBEAN" SERIES

The "Pirates of the Caribbean" series offers a unique perspective on issues of gender and power, illustrating how gender roles and power dynamics can intersect and shape individuals' experiences and opportunities. By examining the journeys of characters like Elizabeth Swann and Tia Dalma/Calypso, we can explore how gender and power intersect and shape the social and political landscape of the series.

The theory of gender and power recognizes that gender is not a fixed or essential category but is shaped by social and cultural norms and expectations. Gender roles and power dynamics are intertwined, with power being unequally distributed based on gender, race, class, and other social identities (SBCC, 2018).

In the "Pirates of the Caribbean" series, gender and power intersect in complex and nuanced ways. Elizabeth Swann's journey from a privileged white woman to a powerful pirate captain and eventually the Pirate King highlights how gender and power are constructed and challenged. Her character's journey reflects the patriarchal and colonial context of the time, where men held the power and non-Western peoples were considered inferior.

Elizabeth's journey also highlights how gender and power intersect with other social identities, such as class and race. As a member of the upper class, she enjoys certain privileges and opportunities that are not available to individuals from lower classes. However, her position as a woman limits her agency and power, reflecting the gender hierarchy that reinforces patriarchal norms and expectations.

Leaders must have empathy and understanding toward marginalized or oppressed people. The "Pirates of the Caribbean" illustrates the importance of seeing beyond appearances and recognizing another's humanity through characters like Tia Dalma/Calypso. Tia Dalma/Calypso's journey, on the other hand, reflects the intersectionality of gender and race. Her character is subjected to the male gaze and is often seen as an "exotic" and "mystical" object, reflecting the racial stereotypes and objectification that non-white individuals faced at the time. Even though Tia Dalma/Calypso is objectified and exoticized by male characters, she refuses to conform to their narrow perceptions. Through her agency and power, she challenges stereotypes and reclaims her identity. She refuses to be defined or controlled by the male characters in the story, demonstrating the importance of asserting one's agency and resisting the constraints imposed by gender and race.

Furthermore, "POTC's" portrayal of piracy as a subversive and anti-authoritarian movement illustrates the potential for challenging traditional power structures and hierarchies. The pirates in the series challenge the authority of the ruling class and the colonialist system, promoting alternative forms of governance and social organization.

Ultimately, the "Pirates of the Caribbean" series offers a unique perspective on the theory of gender and power, illustrating the ways in which gender roles and power dynamics intersect and shape individuals' experiences and opportunities. Their portrayal of characters like Elizabeth Swann and Tia Dalma/Calypso reflects the patriarchal and colonialist context of the time, highlighting the importance of recognizing and challenging multiple forms of discrimination and oppression. By promoting diverse representation and subversive narratives, the "Pirate of Caribbean" series encourages audiences to question traditional power structures and hierarchies and to imagine more equitable and inclusive societies.

A FEMINIST POLITICAL ECOLOGY

A feminist political ecology (FPE) perspective offers a powerful way to analyze gender, power, and the environment. According to the theory, environmental narratives are intertwined with social and political contexts, rather than being objective or neutral (Rocheleau et al., 2013). It is possible to gain insights into how these dynamics shape the social and ecological fabric of the "Pirates of the Caribbean" series by applying FPE to it.

As the series takes place during the 18th century, a period characterized by significant political and economic upheaval, it mirrors the era's colonial power struggles. As the series depicts gender, power, and environmental exploitation, Western powers fiercely compete for control over non-Western territories. From the perspective of FPE, these elements shed light on how colonialism has impacted the environment and gendered power structures.

FPE theory recognizes that the colonialist system is inherently gendered, with men holding the power and women being subjected to various forms of oppression and exploitation. In the "Pirates of the Caribbean" series, gender and power are reflected in the social and ecological landscape of the story.

For example, the series portrays the Caribbean as a resource-rich region that is exploited by Western powers and the ruling class. The environment is viewed as a commodity to be extracted and traded without regard for the long-term consequences or the ecological impact. This exploitation reflects the power dynamics of the colonialist system, where non-Western people and the environment are considered inferior and disposable.

Furthermore, FPE theory recognizes that gender and power intersect with other social identities, such as race and class, to shape individuals' experiences and opportunities. In the "Pirates of the Caribbean" series, characters like Elizabeth Swann and Tia Dalma/Calypso face various forms of oppression and exploitation based on their gender, race, and class. The intersectionality of their social identities illustrates the complex and nuanced ways in which power operates in the colonialist system.

Moreover, FPE theory recognizes that resistance and agency can emerge from the most marginalized and exploited communities. In the "Pirates of the Caribbean" series, the pirates are portrayed as subversive and anti-authoritarian, challenging the power of the ruling class and the colonialist system. The pirates' resistance illustrates the potential for challenging traditional power structures and promoting alternative forms of governance and social organization.

Examining the "Pirates of the Caribbean" series through an FPE lens highlights how gender, power, and the environment intersect and shape the social and ecological landscape of the story. The series reflects the colonialist context of the time, illustrating the importance of recognizing and challenging the gendered and ecological impacts of the colonialist system. By promoting diverse representation and subversive narratives, the Pirates of the Caribbean series encourages audiences to question traditional power structures and imagine more equitable and sustainable societies.

The "Pirates of the Caribbean" provides examples of defiance against societal norms and oppression, illustrating what it means to embrace agency, reclaim power, and subvert the objectification of patriarchal and colonial systems. Elizabeth Swann's transformation from a restrained upper-class woman to a respected pirate captain and eventually the Pirate King exemplifies the transformational power of challenging traditional gender roles. She is an inspirational example of a woman who refuses to conform to societal expectations and carves her own path. Elizabeth Swan disrupts the gender hierarchy as well as promotes gender equality, equity, and diversity through her leadership and defiance. The journey of Tia Dalma/Calypso from objectification to empowerment demonstrates the importance of asserting agency while resisting class and gender hierarchies. Calypso challenges stereotypes and inspires others by reclaiming her power and refusing to be defined by male characters.

Furthermore, the Pirate of the Caribbean explores gender and gender inequality within the context of colonialism and imperialism. Elizabeth Swann's journey reflects the gendered power dynamics of the time, as well as issues of race, class, and sexuality. Taking a critical and argumentative approach to discrimination and oppression, the series highlights the intersectionality of oppression.

In addition to illustrating how gender and power intersect and shape individual experiences and opportunities, the "Pirates of the Caribbean" series offers valuable lessons on gender and power theory. As Elizabeth Swann and Tia Dalma/Calypso navigate complex power structures influenced by gender, race, and class, viewers are inspired to question traditional hierarchies and imagine more equitable societies. As the series recognizes the gendered and ecological effects of colonialism, it encourages audiences to advocate for sustainability and equity.

"Pirates of the Caribbean" goes beyond swashbuckling adventures and promotes meaningful dialog about inclusivity, equity, and empowerment through its inclusion of social issues. With its diverse and compelling narratives, it inspires viewers to break free from societal constraints, challenge oppressive systems, and strive toward a more just and equitable world. As we learn from Elizabeth Swann, Tia Dalma/Calypso, and other women, may we carry their spirit of defiance and resilience into our own journeys toward creating a more inclusive and equitable society.

SUMMARY

As portrayed in the "Pirates of the Caribbean" leaders must recognize the importance of diversity and inclusivity in their teams through breaking down racism and gender inequality. We considered the following:

- Leaders must acknowledge inequality's impact on relationships and demonstrate effective leadership during societal injustices to break barriers.

- Leaders should understand their role and impact on challenging societal norms; embracing strength, resourcefulness, and leadership qualities; and defying gender stereotypes.

- Leaders should be aware of the intersectionality of oppression and how it shapes individual experiences and opportunities.

- Leaders must challenge dysfunctional hierarchies and advocate for diversity, inclusion, and empowerment, encouraging audiences to question traditional power structures.

Having confronted inequalities and provided examples of how Elizabeth Swann and Tia Dalma broke barriers in the "Pirates of the Caribbean" series, in the next chapter, we will explore how effective leadership is affected by the diverse backgrounds, experiences, and needs of each team member.

5

NO TWO PIRATES ARE ALIKE

Leadership is often idealized as the pursuit of perfection – leaders are expected to embody flawless competence and infallibility. However, the "Pirates of the Caribbean" series presents a different perspective, teaching us that flaws and imperfections are not only inevitable but can also enhance leadership effectiveness.

Characters from "Pirates of the Caribbean" capture audiences because of their flaws. Characters are complex, multi-dimensional, and deeply human. These imperfections make them relatable and serve as a reminder that leaders, too, are human. Captain Jack Sparrow exemplifies this theme. He is charming and resourceful but also selfish, opportunistic, and often driven by his vices. Yet, it is these very flaws that make Jack a compelling leader. Pirates, like him, are capable of navigating treacherous waters not because of their perfection, but because of their cunning, resilience, and unconventional thinking.

Captain Jack Sparrow is a central character in the series, and he is a perfect example of this approach to character development. Jack is a witty and charming pirate, but he is also a selfish and opportunistic character who often puts his interests above those of his crew. He also tends to get into trouble and is renowned for his alcoholism and womanizing behavior.

Despite his flaws, Jack is a skilled and resourceful pirate who uses his intelligence and cunning to navigate the dangerous waters of piracy. His fierce loyalty to his crew is one of his redeeming qualities, and he will do anything to protect them, even if it means putting himself in harm's way. Jack's flaws and strengths combine to make him a complex and compelling character that audiences can connect with.

The other characters in the series are also complex and multi-dimensional, adding to the richness of the world-building. Characters like Barbossa and

Blackbeard each have their own set of flaws and strengths that make them engaging and dynamic. Barbossa's ruthlessness and willingness to betray his crew add an element of danger to the story, while Blackbeard's supernatural powers add a fantastical element that heightens the stakes.

TEAM MANAGEMENT SYSTEMS MODEL

The Team Management Systems (TMS) model emphasizes that effective teams are built on a balance of different personality types, each contributing unique strengths to the group's success. The TMS model identifies eight distinct personality types. The Creator is characterized by creativity, imagination, and an unorthodox approach, often generating new ideas and strategies that surprise others – much like how Jack Sparrow uses his imaginative tactics to outmaneuver his enemies. "Pirates of the Caribbean: Dead Man's Chest" is a great example of Jack Sparrow embodying the Creator through his creativity, imagination, and unconventional approach to his life. Jack is pursued by the monstrous Kraken, a seemingly unstoppable force of nature. Instead of confronting it directly, Jack uses his creativity to devise a plan that involves luring the Kraken to attack the Black Pearl while he escapes.

The Explorer thrives on curiosity, adventure, and independence, excelling at exploring new territories and taking risks. As an explorer, Captain Hector Barbossa is driven by a thirst for adventure and a desire to discover new territories. His curiosity and independence are evident in *"Pirates of the Caribbean: On Stranger Tides"* as he embarks on a quest to find the Fountain of Youth. Barbossa's adventurous spirit is reflected in his willingness to take risks, such as striking a dangerous deal with Blackbeard.

The Advancer is enthusiastic, energetic, and sociable, skilled at persuading others and building relationships. In *"Pirates of the Caribbean: Dead Man's Chest,"* as an advancer, James Norrington demonstrates his ability to persuade and influence others, even in difficult circumstances. When Norrington, who has fallen from grace, joins forces with Jack Sparrow and the crew of the Black Pearl, he uses his persuasive skills to navigate the complex relationships between the various factions.

On the other hand, the Assessor is objective, analytical, and logical, adept at evaluating risks and making informed decisions. Elizabeth Swann embodies this role, using her analytical abilities and strong moral compass to guide the crew through morally ambiguous situations. Elizabeth Swann portrays the Assessor in "Pirates of the Caribbean: At World's End" during the pivotal scene when the crew must decide whether to release Calypso, the sea goddess trapped in human form as Tia Dalma. Elizabeth, recognizing the stakes, uses her analytical abilities to weigh the risks and benefits of releasing Calypso. Although the outcome is uncertain, her logical approach and strong moral compass guide her in advocating for the release. As the Assessor, Elizabeth can evaluate the situation objectively and make an informed decision in this morally ambiguous situation. She balances the immediate needs of the crew with the larger, long-term consequences, ultimately influencing the course of events that follow.

The Thruster is determined, driven, and focused, dedicated to achieving goals and getting things done. Blackbeard is an example of a thruster. In *"Pirates of the Caribbean: On Stranger Tides,"* Blackbeard is depicted as a highly driven and ruthless pirate captain who is focused on achieving his goals with unwavering determination. To find the Fountain of Youth, he is willing to use dark magic and manipulate those around him to ensure his immortality. Thruster personality is characterized by Blackbeard's relentless pursuit of survival as he focuses on achieving his objectives at any cost.

The Concluder is cautious, systematic, and practical, excelling in planning and organizing – qualities that Will Turner exemplifies with his methodical nature and technical skills, ensuring the crew's plans are executed efficiently. In *"Pirates of the Caribbean: The Curse of the Black Pearl"* when Will, realizing that Jack is the key to rescuing Elizabeth Swann from the pirates, uses his skills to help free Jack Sparrow from his chains using his blacksmithing expertise. In addition to providing stability and practicality to the crew's plans, Will's ability to plan and organize complex tasks with precision and care underscores his role as the Concluder.

The Upholder is reliable, responsible, and conscientious, proficient in following rules and procedures. As an officer in the Royal Navy, Norrington is reliable, responsible, and conscientious, strictly adhering to rules and procedures. Despite falling from grace in Dead Man's Chest, Norrington's desire to regain his honor drives him to retrieve the heart of Davy Jones, demonstrating his deep commitment to the principles he upholds.

Finally, the Maintainer is cooperative, supportive, and diplomatic, playing a crucial role in mediating and resolving conflicts within the team

(Hedges, 1990; Margerison et al., 1986). Governor Weatherby Swann (Elizabeth's father) serves as a maintainer. In *The Curse of the "Black Pearl and Dead Man's Chest"* Governor Swann is cooperative, supportive, and diplomatic. His role involves mediating and resolving conflicts, often trying to maintain peace and order in Port Royal despite the chaos of pirates.

By recognizing and harnessing these diverse personality traits, teams can achieve a balanced dynamic that enhances overall performance and success. By recognizing and harnessing these diverse personality traits, teams can achieve a balanced dynamic that enhances overall performance and success.

For a team to be successful, it is important to have a balance of these different personality types. Each type brings its unique strengths and abilities to the table. For example, a team may need a visionary leader, a practical organizer, a creative problem solver, and a diplomatic mediator to succeed.

SOCIAL EXCHANGE THEORY

The diverse roles identified by the TMS model are most effective when they are supported by the principles of Social Exchange Theory. The Creator thrives when other team members, such as the Assessor and the Concluder, acknowledge and build upon their innovative ideas. An Upholder or Maintainer is more likely to be effective if they perceive that their efforts in ensuring stability and conflict resolution are appreciated and acknowledged.

One theory that is relevant when it comes to creating a positive work environment is Social Exchange Theory. This theory proposes that relationships are based on a give-and-take exchange of resources such as time, energy, and support. When people perceive that they are receiving more resources than they are giving, they are more likely to be committed to the relationship (Cook et al., 2013).

By illustrating the importance of understanding individual strengths and weaknesses, the series emphasizes the importance of understanding individual strengths and weaknesses.

MASLOW'S HIERARCHY OF NEEDS

Maslow's Hierarchy of Needs (Maslow, 1943) is a psychological framework that proposes a pyramid of needs, from the most basic survival needs at the bottom to achieving personal fulfillment at the top. The story of "Pirates of the Caribbean" provides a vivid and relatable lens through which we can explore these needs.

NAVIGATING MASLOW'S HIERARCHY OF NEEDS WITH PIRATES

"Pirates of the Caribbean" may seem like a tale of lawless pirates, cursed treasure, and epic sea battles, but beneath the surface is an exploration of human desire, need, and fulfillment. Our journey through these hazardous waters will take us through Maslow's Hierarchy's five tiers – physiological needs, safety needs, love and belonging needs, esteem needs, and self-actualization – and we'll see how charismatic Captain Jack Sparrow and his motley crew of pirates help us understand them.

Captain Jack Sparrow and his crew travel through the pirate world, discovering not only gold and jewels but also hidden treasures of leadership and human needs. The content of this chapter will take you on an exhilarating journey through the Pirates of the Caribbean movie series, which carries not only the scent of salt but also an analysis of Maslow's Hierarchy of Needs.

Abraham Maslow developed his psychological theory in the mid-20th century. Hierarchy of Needs is a psychological concept developed to explain individual needs. Despite its primary psychological roots, this theory has important implications for leadership in that it enables leaders to understand the needs and motivations of individuals (Huitt, 2007).

The Maslow Hierarchy of Needs divides human needs into five levels, starting with the most basic and progressing to the highest level. Physiological needs, such as food, water, and shelter, are essential for survival. Once these are met, safety needs emerge, focusing on security and stability. Next, individuals seek belongingness and love, forming relationships and connections. The next step is achieving self-esteem, which involves self-confidence, achievement, and recognition. Self-actualization is at the top, where individuals strive to achieve their full potential through personal growth and fulfillment.

The Maslow Hierarchy of Needs provides an effective model for managers and leaders to explain psychological needs and motivations within a group or organization. By implementing this theory into their leadership practices, effective leaders can create a supportive, motivating workplace that thrives and helps employees reach their full potential.

A supportive, motivating workplace that thrives and helps employees reach their full potential can be enhanced if leaders use differentiated leadership, and motivation, based on Maslow's theory. Leaders can adapt their leadership style to meet the needs of team members at different levels in the hierarchy. Leadership may provide more guidance and support to someone struggling with safety needs while giving more autonomy to someone seeking self-actualization. Using Maslow's theory, leaders can discover what motivates their team members. Some people may be motivated primarily by the desire for recognition and achievement (esteem needs), while others may be driven by the desire for personal growth (self-actualization).

As with other leaders, Captain Jack Sparrow also demonstrates leadership practices based on Maslow's hierarchy of needs on his journey with his crew. With "Pirates of the Caribbean's" wisdom, leaders and team managers will better understand the profound connection between the pursuit of adventure, freedom, and self-expression, and our human needs.

Physiological Needs: Satisfying the Cravings of the Soul

Physiological needs are at the base of Maslow's pyramid, the most basic requirement for survival. Imagine, if you will, the endless expanse of the open sea, the creaking of the beams, and the call of gulls as we find ourselves aboard the Black Pearl. In "Pirates of the Caribbean: The Curse of the Black Pearl," amidst the swaying masts and salty sea breeze, Jack's parched lips and bleary eyes spoke volumes about his longing for that sweet nectar of the sea (and, of course, food and water too!).

Of course, Captain Jack Sparrow's insatiable desire for rum becomes a symbolic representation of our most fundamental cravings in "Pirates of the Caribbean: The Curse of the Black Pearl." The longing Jack has for that sweet nectar of the sea reflects our own primal needs for nourishment, shelter, and safety. Jack reminds us that fulfilling our physiological needs is the foundation for all other aspirations. A sailor asks a question everyone has been thinking about, but not dared to ask. Everyone is waiting for Jack's answer anxiously as if anticipating a significant revelation or decision that could impact them all since the answer could have serious implications.

As the moonlight danced on the restless waves, Jack found himself surrounded by his loyal crew aboard the Black Pearl. They had just concluded a treacherous battle, emerging victorious but not unscathed. The crew, weary and hungry, gathered around their charismatic captain, their eyes fixated on the infamous bottle of rum, which had dwindled to a mere trickle.

A sly grin tugged at the corner of Jack's lips as he turned to face his crew, his eyes shining mischievously beneath the shadow of his tricorn hat. His words drew a chuckle from the weary souls around him, who were glad for the momentary diversion from their aching muscles and empty bellies. The crew erupted in laughter, their worries momentarily forgotten in the shared camaraderie of the moment.

This humorous exchange between the captain and crew illustrates a profound truth – the importance of fulfilling our basic needs. Jack's insatiable desire for rum mirrors our own primal urges for sustenance, shelter, and safety. Just as even the most cunning pirate cannot set sail without food, water, and a sturdy vessel, we, too, require these fundamental necessities to navigate the unpredictable seas of life.

So, whether you find yourself amidst the crashing waves of the Caribbean or in the vast expanse of the modern world, remember the wisdom of Captain Jack Sparrow. Embrace the understanding that, just like rum to a pirate, fulfilling our physiological needs is the cornerstone upon which all other aspirations can flourish.

Safety Needs: Balancing on the Edge of Uncertainty

Moving up the hierarchy, we encounter safety needs, a realm fraught with danger and uncertainty. In the swashbuckling world of the Pirates of the Caribbean, safety is a precious commodity, perpetually under siege by rival pirates, mythical sea creatures, and the allure of cursed treasure. One particular scene from "Pirates of the Caribbean: Dead Man's Chest" vividly captures the perilous nature of Jack Sparrow's existence.

Captain Jack found himself in the throes of a relentless pursuit as the Black Pearl sailed through treacherous waters. The Kraken, a monstrous sea creature with tentacles that could crush a ship in its grip, lurked beneath the dark depths, its insatiable hunger driving it to claim its next victim.

Tension filled the air as the crew scrambled to ready the cannons, their eyes darting between the approaching behemoth and their charismatic captain. Unruffled by the imminent threat, Jack strolled across the deck, his trademark swagger undiminished despite the gravity of the situation.

The crew caught between the awe-inspiring sight of the Kraken and Jack's philosophical musings, exchanging glances tinged with trepidation and admiration. They were reminded that safety, in their tumultuous world, was a fleeting notion, forever at odds with the irresistible allure of discovery and freedom.

During their fateful encounter with the Kraken, the Black Pearl and her crew displayed the precarious balance between safety and adventure. A cunning pirate like Captain Jack Sparrow knew that safety was a fleeting concept, constantly at risk from the sea's dangers. The Kraken's attack highlights the harsh reality that even the most calculated plans can be thwarted by the unpredictable forces of nature.

And so, as we navigate our lives, it is worth remembering Jack's words: that safety is but a flickering flame in a world teeming with danger. In embracing the uncertainty, in venturing into the unknown, we find the true essence of life and the courage to sail through the stormy seas of existence.

Belongings and Love Needs: Finding Companionship in the Midst of Chaos

As we ascend Maslow's Hierarchy, we arrive at the love and belongingness needs, where the importance of social connections takes center stage. In the epic "Pirates of the Caribbean" movies, the bonds forged among pirates are as vital as the wind in their sails. Captain Jack Sparrow, a master of unconventional alliances, knows all too well the significance of forming close-knit crews to navigate the treacherous waters of the high seas.

In "Pirates of the Caribbean: At World's End," as the fate of the pirate brethren hangs in the balance, Elizabeth Swann, a formidable and determined pirate herself, finds herself in a perilous situation. Seeking an ally amidst the chaos, she approaches the notorious Captain Barbossa, her voice laced with urgency and determination.

Barbossa, a seasoned pirate with a checkered past, surveys the tumultuous scene with concern and resolve. The air crackles with a shared understanding between the two pirates, their words echoing the universal human desire for companionship, acceptance, and a place to belong. They both know that in a world of shifting allegiances and cutthroat ambition, the bonds of trust and camaraderie are the very lifeblood of their existence.

The scene unfolds against a backdrop of chaos and uncertainty as pirates from different corners of the globe assemble, drawn together by a shared cause. They form a mosaic of unique individuals, each possessing distinct skills and quirks but united by the unspoken understanding that their strength lies in their collective resolve.

As the camera pans across the motley crew, it captures fleeting glances of recognition, nods of solidarity, and shared determination etched on weathered faces. These pirates, once strangers, now stand shoulder to shoulder, ready to face the gallows or whatever perils lie ahead.

Elizabeth's words convey the deep human need for connection and belonging. As she points out, no matter how challenging life is or how dangerous the sea is, people yearn for companionship, loyalty, and unconditional support. A trusted group of allies can be a source of strength and comfort, especially during difficult times.

And so, we learn from Elizabeth Swann and her pirate brethren that in the pursuit of love and belongingness, we must find our crew – a tribe of kindred spirits who will navigate the storms beside us, defy the odds, and remind us that even amidst the chaos, we are never alone.

Esteem Needs: Dueling for Reputation and Respect

Continuing our ascent through the hierarchy, we arrive at the esteem needs, where pirates and their swashbuckling exploits take center stage. Within the thrilling realm of the "Pirates of the Caribbean," the quest for recognition and respect becomes a tantalizing prize sought by those who roam the high seas. One memorable scene from "Pirates of the Caribbean: The Curse of the Black Pearl" perfectly captures the interplay of reputation and esteem among these audacious buccaneers.

A tense conversation takes place between Captain Jack Sparrow and Captain Barbossa amid flickering candlelight in the Black Pearl's captain's quarters. Barbossa challenges Jack's plan to retrieve the cursed treasure, suggesting Jack's confidence might be misplaced. Barbossa's retort momentarily cracks Jack's confident facade, revealing the ongoing struggle for control and dominance between the two captains.

The weight of those words hangs in the air, challenging Jack's reputation as a fearless and courageous captain. Barbossa's deliberate choice of language strikes at the core of Jack's quest for esteem, insinuating that venturing into uncharted territories exposes him to perils that cast doubt upon his legendary status.

Undeterred by the threat and armed with his trademark wit, Jack counters with a sly grin. His retort, veiled in bravado and a touch of irony, subtly reasserts his confidence, refusing to let the shadow of doubt tarnish his reputation.

The exchange between the two captains illustrates the delicate dance of reputation and respect within the pirate realm. Their words are not merely a clash of egos; they represent the eternal struggle for esteem and recognition in a world where one's worth is measured by daring exploits and feats of audacity.

For these swashbucklers, reputation is the currency that shapes their interactions and elevates them within the pirate hierarchy. They crave the admiration and respect of their peers, understanding that their very survival depends on the perception of their skill, courage, and cunning.

Jack Sparrow's reputation precedes him in this sea-faring world, where legends are born and myths are forged. His reputation is built upon daring escapes, audacious maneuvers, and an unyielding spirit. To question that reputation is to strike at the very heart of Jack's esteem needs, forcing him to prove his mettle once more.

As the scene fades, leaving the echoes of their verbal jousting behind, the significance of esteem and reputation resonates beyond the realm of pirates. It reminds us that, like the ocean's tides, our worth is subject to the opinions and perceptions of others.

It prompts us to reflect upon the importance of cultivating our reputation and earning our peers' respect and esteem. In doing so, we carve a path that leads us to our own version of uncharted horizons, where the monsters of doubt and uncertainty dare not tread.

Self-actualization: Embracing the Freedom of Self-expression

Finally, we find ourselves at the pinnacle of Maslow's Hierarchy: self-actualization, where individuals pursue their full potential and strive for personal fulfillment. In the spirited world of the "Pirates of the Caribbean" series, there is no better embodiment of this pursuit than the enigmatic Captain Jack Sparrow. With his unruly hair, smudged eyeliner, and

unwavering spirit, Jack stands as a living testament to the boundless yearning for freedom and self-expression.

In the midst of a moonlit escapade aboard a weathered ship sailing through
the star-studded canvas of the night sky, Jack finds himself contemplating the
essence of his existence as he addresses his loyal crew, the sea breeze tugs at
his dreadlocked mane, his voice carrying a mixture of longing and defiance.

His crew, a diverse assemblage of misfits and dreamers, exchange
glances, their faces illuminated by the flickering glow of torches. They are
both perplexed and awestruck by their captain's unwavering devotion to
the uncharted path he has chosen. Jack in his speeches mirrors their hidden
desires, the yearning to break free from the constraints of society and sail
toward the horizon of their true selves.

The crew listens in rapt attention, their hearts stirred by Jack's words as he
continues to paint a vivid picture of self-actualization. Throughout his speeches,
Jack Sparrow appeals to his crew's desires for freedom, adventure, and personal gain. This helps them reach their full potential or self-actualization. Even
when faced with overwhelming odds, he can get his crew to rally around these
motivations. He often frames dangerous missions as opportunities for glory or
wealth, which inspires loyalty and enthusiasm among the crew.

He speaks of daring escapades, unexpected alliances, and the relentless
pursuit of one's truth. The air becomes charged with a shared understanding that each crew member has a unique path to tread and journey toward
personal fulfillment.

Jack's proclamation reverberates through the night, a rallying cry for all
who yearn to live on their terms. Captain Jack Sparrow embodies the very
essence of self-actualization in his unyielding spirit and refusal to be confined
by societal expectations.

And so, as we navigate the uncharted waters of our lives, let us take a
page from Jack's book, embracing the chaos and forging our destinies. Let
us listen to the whispers of our hearts and venture forth, unafraid to be true
to ourselves. For it is in the pursuit of self-actualization that we unlock the
treasures hidden within and, like Captain Jack Sparrow, sail toward the horizon of our greatest adventures.

So there we have it, Maslow's Hierarchy of Needs, as seen through the
lens of the "Pirates of the Caribbean" series. From basic physiological needs
to self-actualization, these themes are interwoven within the adventures of
Captain Jack Sparrow and his pirate brethren. Remember, as you navigate

the seas of life, keep your compass pointed toward fulfilling those needs, and you'll discover your treasure trove of personal growth and fulfillment!

We explored the most basic of human desires – the physiological need for sustenance and survival – to the ultimate aspirations of self-actualization. Throughout the series, Captain Jack Sparrow's adventures have served as a captivating backdrop for illustrating each level of the hierarchy with wit, charm, and an unrelenting spirit of exploration.

As Captain Jack Sparrow pursues self-actualization, he becomes the embodiment of the unburdened embrace of one's true self. In his journey, we are reminded that personal growth and fulfillment often lie in charting our own course, dancing with fate, and living a life that resonates with the core of our being. Leaders can learn from Jack's resolve to forge his own path and encourage their teams to do the same.

Just as in our professional lives, reputation and reputation management are essential in the pirate realm. In the verbal battle between Jack Sparrow and Captain Barbossa, we see the importance of cultivating our reputation and earning the respect of our peers. It is important to recognize that our worth is often determined by our daring exploits and audacious feats. In order to empower and uplift our teams, we must acknowledge their accomplishments and foster an environment where recognition and respect are readily granted.

Bonds among pirates vividly depict love and belonging, the desire for social connections. Through Captain Jack Sparrow's ability to form unconventional alliances and create close-knit crews, we learn that companionship, acceptance, and belonging are universal human desires. Leadership means creating an environment where teams feel accepted, valued, and supported, allowing them to achieve their best.

Life itself is a thrilling dance between the allure of discovery and the comfort of security, a realm fraught with danger and uncertainty. Pirates navigate treacherous waters, and we, too, must navigate uncertainties in business and life. We must encourage our teams to embrace the unknown, venture into uncharted territories, and find the courage to sail through stormy waters.

Physiological needs are the basis for Maslow's Hierarchy – the most basic survival requirements. Captain Jack Sparrow's insatiable thirst for rum serves as a reminder of our primal needs for sustenance, shelter, and safety. Leadership requires ensuring our teams have the support they need to flourish in a stable environment.

The adventures of Captain Jack Sparrow and his crew illuminate the path to personal growth and fulfillment, emphasizing the importance of fulfilling our needs and striving for self-actualization. Our leadership compasses should always point toward fulfilling the needs of our teams and ourselves, just as Jack's compass does.

"Pirates of the Caribbean" is a captivating world filled with courage, camaraderie, and chaos. We've seen how these themes are woven into their exciting adventures through the lens of Maslow's hierarchy. By taking these lessons from the high seas and applying them to our own leadership journeys, we can unlock the treasure trove of personal growth and fulfillment that lies within us. Embrace adventure, cultivate your reputation, nurture the bonds of belongingness, and chart a course toward self-actualization. As a result, not only will you lead your crew to success, but you will also find your own path to leadership excellence.

Now that we've reached the end of our journey with the pirates and their quest for fulfillment, it's time to look back and reflect on our discoveries. At the end of the final chapter, we'll tie together the lessons learned and formulate a plan for applying the newfound wisdom to our own leadership journeys.

EMBRACING IMPERFECTIONS: LESSONS FROM THE PIRATES

Lesson 1: Relatability Through Vulnerability

It is one of the key lessons from "Pirates of the Caribbean" that flaws make leaders more relatable. When leaders are often placed on pedestals, showing vulnerability can bridge the gap between them and their followers. Despite his frequent mistakes and unconventional methods, Jack Sparrow is a figure that others can identify with. His vulnerabilities invite empathy and support, creating a strong bond with his crew. A leader's ability to demonstrate vulnerability can foster trust and open communication, essential elements for teamwork and leadership.

Lesson 2: Innovation and Creativity

Creativity and innovation are often sparked by imperfections. Sparrow's unorthodox thinking and spontaneous decision-making often lead to innovative solutions and unexpected successes. As a result of his unconventional approach, he can think outside the box. By embracing their flaws, leaders can inspire creativity and innovation within their teams. Leaders can encourage creative problem-solving by embracing diverse perspectives and acknowledging their own limitations.

Lesson 3: Authenticity and Trust

Flaws contribute to a leader's authenticity. Authentic leaders are transparent about their strengths and weaknesses. Characters in "Pirates of the Caribbean" are trustworthy and credible because they are authentic, flaws, and all. Followers are more likely to trust leaders who are honest about their imperfections. Building a loyal and committed team requires trust. Authenticity fosters a culture where team members feel safe to express themselves and contribute their best efforts.

Lesson 4: Resilience and Growth

Embracing flaws also promotes resilience and growth. As "Pirates of the Caribbean" progresses, each character learns from their mistakes and grows stronger as a result. Sparrow's numerous escapes from dire situations illustrate the importance of resilience. Acknowledging flaws makes leaders more receptive to feedback and self-improvement. As a result of this growth mindset, they can adapt to changing environments and thrive in them, allowing them to turn setbacks into opportunities for growth.

Lesson 5: Building Diverse and Complementary Teams

"Pirates of the Caribbean" shows that no two pirates are alike, and their flaws often complement each other. Captain Barbossa's strategic thinking balances Captain Jack Sparrow's resourcefulness, while Elizabeth Swann's loyalty and bravery complement Captain Hector Barbossa's cunning. Leaders must recognize and appreciate the strengths and weaknesses of each member of their teams. Creating diverse, complementary teams allows us to leverage the strengths of individuals while compensating for their weaknesses, leading to a more effective team.

Lesson 6: Empathy and Understanding

Character flaws in "Pirates of the Caribbean" also teach us the importance of empathy and understanding in leadership. Jack Sparrow's tendency to prioritize his own interests often leads to conflict with his crew. However, his ability to empathize with their motivations and desires allows him to rally their support when necessary. Leaders must recognize that everyone has flaws and struggles. Creating an environment where individuals feel valued and motivated to contribute their best requires empathy and understanding.

The "Pirates of the Caribbean" series reminds us that effective leadership does not require perfection. Embracing flaws can enhance a leader's relatability, creativity, authenticity, and resilience. By recognizing and leveraging their imperfections, leaders can build stronger connections with their teams, foster innovation, and navigate challenges more efficiently. In a world where flawlessness is often emphasized, it's important to remember that no two leaders are alike, and it is their unique imperfections that make them effective. The series reminds us that flaws and imperfections should be embraced and utilized for effective leadership.

SUMMARY

It is important to remember that leadership doesn't require perfection. This requires understanding one's own flaws and those of others, adaptability, and the wisdom to harness diverse strengths within a team. Leadership that embraces imperfection inspires both growth and innovation in their teams. Let us embrace our flaws and embark on our leadership journey in pirate spirit. Knowing that no two pirates are alike, and our imperfections can be our greatest strengths. This chapter considered the following:

- Leaders need to understand the strengths and weaknesses of their team members.

- Understanding team members allows for effective delegation of tasks and ensures that each member contributes optimally to team success.

- Leaders should create a positive work environment where team members feel valued, respected, and appreciated.

- It is the leader's responsibility to ensure the well-being of his or her team.

- Leaders need to strike a balance between the need for security and the need for innovation and risk-taking.

- Leaders need to create a culture of cohesiveness and support among their teams.

- Leaders need to acknowledge achievements and build respect among team members.

- The role of leaders should be to encourage continuous development in both personal and professional areas.

As we recognize the individuality of each pirate, it's crucial to stay true to our own path despite the diversity. We will explore the age-old practice of parley in the next chapter, learning how communication can bridge gaps and build stronger connections.

6

LEARNING HOW TO PARLEY

In the "Pirates of the Caribbean" series, the characters talk about the "Pirate Code" and the practice known as "parley" (or "parlay") in a humorous tongue-in-cheek manner. But, in fact, the Pirate Code is not made up for the movies as real-world pirates did have a Pirate Codex (Allende, 2018; Cordingly, 2013) that specified the terms of parley, or a manner in which pirates communicated and negotiated.

In this chapter, we will consider the practice of parley. We will define what it is in the terms of a pirate's life and consider how it can be used in modern organizations. We will consider how parley was used in "Pirates of the Caribbean," by real-world pirates, and how it relates to negotiation as well as how leaders might approach communicating with others.

WHAT IS PARLEY?

Parley is derived from the French word "parle," meaning to speak. In "Pirates of the Caribbean," the practice of parley is invoked several times throughout the films. In one example, Elizabeth Swann calls for a parley when she is captured by Barbossa's crew. In several situations, invoking parley is done by characters in "Pirates of the Caribbean" when they were in trouble. In each use, characters leverage this communication tactic to attempt to negotiate for their best interests.

The use of parley occurs because it causes a stop in action. While it is used as a stall tactic in the "Pirates of the Caribbean" movies, it can and should be used to start a discussion or negotiation as per its historical intent. The practice of parley, especially in its function as starting a discussion, has been useful both in historical contexts as well as in our modern organizations.

HISTORICAL PARLEYS

While "Pirates of the Caribbean" includes the concept of "parley" in a comedic sense, there have been several instances of using parley among historic pirates including (33rd Square, 2023):

- Black Bart used parley to create partnerships with other pirates
- Captain Henry Morgan leveraged parley to get Spanish sailors to surrender without a fight
- Blackbeard similarly invoked parley to negotiate with merchant crews to give up their cargo

It would be great if modern organizations would also follow suit. If they would, organizations would see the benefit of stopping in the middle of a decision or heated discussion to slow the choice down. In these above pirate examples, stopping to engage in a formal dialog helped to negotiate positive outcomes that resulted in minimal violence. Leveraging parley in modern organizations could likewise do the same by allowing multiple parties to be heard and acknowledged. Thus, the practice of parley could help with improving both negotiation and communication style in organizations.

RELATIONSHIP TO NEGOTIATION

As noted, pirate parleys (both fictional and non-fictional) cause a break in action and signal that a formal communication is requested. So often in organizations, people "do things" without communicating to others the purpose of their actions. Because of this, less than optimal decisions might be made that could harm organizations. But, by asking for a formal "parley" another party knows that important negotiations will be forthcoming.

There is a lot of work from a leadership and organizational standpoint on what negotiations is and this section will be a broad simplification without much of the nuance and complexity of negotiations as, indeed, techniques for negotiating can fill an entire book. In short, negotiations can basically be defined as any form of communication in which parties try to acquire something out of the discussion.

Of course, negotiations can occur over a number of things that parties hope to acquire. These could include (but are not limited to):

- Compensation

- Budget

- Headcount

- Resources

- Promotion opportunities

- Title

While these are but some of the things that are negotiated upon in modern real-world organizations, the characters in "Pirates of the Caribbean" also haggle over such similar resources. Jack Sparrow and Hector Barbossa spar throughout the films as to who is the true Captain (title) of the Black Pearl. The Brethren Court meets, in part, to figure out how to best unite their crews (i.e., headcount for the crews themselves and resources regarding ships) to take back control of the sea. And, certainly, pirates wouldn't be pirates if they weren't often looking for some type of treasure (compensation).

In these instances in the films, just as in our organizations, leaders may engage in distributive or integrative approaches (Barry & Friedman, 1998). A distributive approach is a perspective focused on winning and losing. One party is the winner and the other is the loser because it is perceived that there is only a small number of whatever the parties are negotiating on. There is, after all, only so much budget or so much treasure to go around. One pirate (perhaps the captain) may get a large portion of the gold and the others get what is left.

On the other hand, an integrative approach seeks to think outside of the box regarding how to negotiate. Rather than focus on a win/lose or us/them scenario, those that leverage an integrative perspective seek to create solutions that will be useful for everyone. These types of negotiators try to expand the resources that they are discussing rather than focus on just a few limited fixed resources. While one pirate still gets a portion of the gold, the negotiators broaden their topic from just gold to other things for which they can bargain.

In "Pirates of the Caribbean," Davy Jones seems to be distributive in nature. The resources that he focuses on are the number of years that his crew owes him. With many interactions he has with his crew (or would-be crew), he focuses on the length of time that they will become part of The Flying Dutchman. He does not consider anything else in his negotiations with his crew other than how long they will serve him on his ship.

On the other hand, Jack Sparrow seems to be more integrative in nature. When he is in a bind, Jack negotiates by suggesting he has additional information that he could share, indicating that he knows the whereabouts of treasure, or reframing the situation to make his negotiating partners rethink their decisions. In doing so, Sparrow does not focus on a limited number of resources on which to discuss.

Of course, which type of negotiating approach is more successful depends on a number of things. First, it depends on the focus of the other party – is that person more distributive or integrative in nature? Second, is it possible to be integrative or are the resources truly limited so that distributive is the most appropriate? This, of course, would depend on if the other party is narrowly focused on only one resource in which to bargain. And, third, what is the other party's preferred communication style? Each person likely has a preferred communication style that might make them either more or less comfortable in distributive or integrative negotiations.

COMMUNICATION TYPE AND STYLE

How someone approaches parleys and negotiations could depend largely on their communication styles. While there are many ways to classify different communication styles, one useful approach classifies communication styles into three types (Fairhurst, 2010; O'Keefe, 1988): expressive, conventional, and strategic.

Each of these types is related to how a communicator would "frame" their message. To frame a message means to provide meaning in a certain way that audiences may understand it (Fairhurst, 2005). Each person (including fictional pirates) is often most comfortable with one of these types.

The first type of communication style is expressive (Fairhurst, 2010; O'Keefe, 1988). These types of communicators basically say anything without much thought to how they communicate the message. In some ways, Will Turner communicates in this manner, especially early on in the series. When audiences first meet him, he tends to be naïve in the types of things he says and communicates. Despite being low born, he outwardly expresses his love for Elizabeth Swann who is high born. And he furthermore confronts Jack Sparrow early in "Curse of the Black Pearl" despite not being a skilled swordsman himself. Both of these examples suggest an expressive style because Turner is basically communicating whatever comes to his mind. Over time, though, throughout the films Turner changes his style and, as he does so, becomes more effective in leading others and accomplishing his goals. As one might suspect, individuals who are expressive may not always be satisfied with how successful they are in influencing others over time.

The second communication type is conventional (Fairhurst, 2010; O'Keefe, 1988) and these individuals attempt to fit in within the norms of what a social group expects. James Norrington often communicates in a conventional manner. As a leader of the British navy, he plays the part of Jack Sparrow's foil. He is structured in his approach to interacting with his crew and with others just as one might expect from a leader of a colonial naval fleet. He seems to follow formal procedure when communicating with Weatherby Swann, Governor of Port Royal. He is adamant in chasing and defeating pirates and the way he talks about it seems in line with what would be expected of an officer in the Navy. Like Norrington, leaders that follow this kind of style tend to be successful when they're dealing with people that think alike.

Someone who leverages the third approach (strategic) communicates in such a way that fits with a variety of different audiences and often adjusts their approach to talking based on who they're talking to. Captain Jack Sparrow is very convincing because he adjusts his approach depending on who he's talking with. To Will Turner, Sparrow communicates in a way that suggests that he can help him to find Elizabeth Swann. To Captain Barbossa, Sparrow communicates that he can help him break the curse that plagues his crew. Jack Sparrow's ultimate goal is to win back the Black Pearl. Helping, working with, and communicating effectively to Barbossa and Turner will move Sparrow closer to his own goals. In our modern organizations as well, those individuals that are most strategic tend to be effective in leading multiple groups.

And, of course, there is a link here to negotiation. Those that are able to influence multiple groups and adapt their communication styles (strategics) to fit a variety of situations may be more effective at negotiations.

SUMMARY

An important part of being a leader (and being a pirate) is communicating. This chapter explored communication in a variety of ways.

- The pirate practice of "parley" stops action and allows a conversation to occur. The idea is ultimately to engage in some form of negotiations.

- The practice of parley has been useful for historic pirates and, because it forces a conversation, it can be beneficial in modern organizations to discuss/negotiate resources.

- While pirates can negotiate on their cut of treasure, there are a variety of things that modern organizational leaders will negotiate on as well.

- How successful a leader or pirate captain is with negotiating may depend on their communication style which could be expressive, conventional, or strategic.

Having learned the skills of dialog and negotiation, we realize that no two pirates – or people – are alike. In the next chapter, we will learn how to let your inner compass guide you through uncharted waters, ensuring you stay true to your values and vision.

7

LETTING YOUR COMPASS GUIDE YOU

One of the major things that all leaders must do is make decisions. Of course, many of the best decisions are those that are made using some set of ethics or values. Just as in the real world, characters in "Pirates of the Caribbean" illustrate how leaders and captains leverage values, ethics, and morals in their decisions.

Leaders also make decisions that help their organizations achieve their goals. Throughout the films, Jack Sparrow has a compass that at first glance doesn't seem to work. But the compass really points to whatever he desires most – and those desires, of course, could be the goals that a leader hopes to achieve or those things that a leader values most. This chapter considers how leaders leverage both values and goals.

TRUE NORTH: VALUES AND GOALS

Values and goals both drive decisions. Leaders and captains often based their decisions on things that are of importance to them and both values and goals can guide decisions. Values are related to ideals or morals that someone cares about (Cambridge Dictionary, n.d.). Goals, on the other hand, are desired end states. They are what a group of people hopes to accomplish (Elliott & Dweck, 1988). Of course, it may be easier to accomplish certain goals if all crew members are on board with and accept the goals toward which they are working.

According to the Rokeach values approach (Tuulik et al., 2016), there are two types of values, one of which is similar to the concept of goals. The type of values similar to goals is known as terminal values. Terminal values are things that people care about that they hope to achieve. Thus, they are desired end states. These are things that individuals work toward and could include outcomes like peace, respect, prosperity, and virtually any other result. Instrumental values, on the other hand, represent things that people care about that help them to achieve their terminal values. In other words, these are ways of behaving that help achieve desired end states and can be thought of as behaviors that evidence things such as hard work, honesty, charisma, and many other ways of acting.

The point here is this: both values (what we care about) and goals (desired end states) guide the decisions of captains and leaders. As such, it would be ideal for leaders to understand what they most care about in order to make deliberate decisions that can best leverage particular values and can work toward achieving specific outcomes. In other words, leaders must be able to reflect upon and articulate their deepest cares so that they know them well to best act on them.

UNDERSTAND WHAT YOU CARE ABOUT

In the "Pirates of the Caribbean" series, different characters care about different things which influence their actions. Interestingly, enough, the compass (possessed throughout the series mostly by Jack Sparrow but also by different characters at some points in time) that appears to be broken throughout most of the first parts of the franchise actually points to whatever the character that possesses it cares most about.

For characters in "Pirates of the Caribbean," this is a very tangible way that they are reminded about their values and goals. This physical reminder of the compass pointing the direction toward their deepest desire can help them remember what they are working toward as they deliberately make decisions that lead them in the direction of their most important cares.

Unfortunately, real-world leaders are unlikely to possess such a device that serves as a reminder to make decisions in line with one's values. Thus, it is important for leaders to be able to constantly reflect on what they care about. These can be their goals or the terminal values that they hope to accomplish. By this constant reflection, leaders will be more attuned to their deepest cares and make decisions accordingly.

If leaders can articulate what they care about, that means that they understand their goals and their values. And, if they understand their goals and their values, they will deliberately make choices in line with them.

MOTIVATION AND GOAL SETTING THEORY

Reflecting on what one cares about helps to motivate a leader to make decisions in line with their values and goals. Likewise, if their own personal values and goals match those of their crew, leaders and captains will also motivate their followers to accomplish the mission and vision of their organization.

There are two basic types of motivators, intrinsic and extrinsic (Ryan & Deci, 2000). Intrinsic motivators are those things that come from within. They could include personal drive or ambition. Some people might be motivated to engage in a behavior because they really enjoy the task. In "Pirates of the Caribbean," Will Turner is often motivated by his feelings that come from within. He is motivated to find Elizzabeth because of his love for her and he is motivated to become a part of Davy Jones' crew in order to save his father out of love for him.

Extrinsic motivation, on the other hand, is something that comes from outside of someone. Extrinsic motivators are often thought of as tangible or physical rewards. For the pirates in "Pirates of the Caribbean," there are a number of physical and tangible rewards that the pirates are motivated to pursue. For example, in various installments of the series, the pirates are motivated to pursue a treasure of Aztec gold, a dead man's chest (Verbinski, 2006), and the Fountain of Youth among other extrinsic motivators that guide their behaviors.

Captains should understand the values and goals of their crew and ensure that they are aligned with their own personal values and goals. Once done, leaders will want to consider how best to motivate their followers to obtain those goals. Goal setting theory can be considered to help leaders guide followers' behaviors.

Goal setting theory has several major components (Locke & Latham, 2019). Among them are the concepts of specificity, difficulty, acceptance, and feedback. Goal specificity is how clear a goal is. Goal difficulty is how challenging a goal is. Goal acceptance is how much followers buy-in to a goal. Finally, goal feedback is how much knowledge a person performing a task has in understanding how they are doing related to accomplishing a goal. The theory goes that if these attributes can be increased, then motivation and thereby performance would be increased. In the case of difficulty, the goal would need to be challenging enough without being impossible, of course.

Goal setting theory is illustrated several times throughout the "Pirates of the Caribbean" series. When Barbossa leads his crew to find the Aztec gold in "The Curse of the Black Pearl," goal setting theory can explain the crew's behavior. The goal is clear (specificity) – the crew knows that they are searching for the treasure to break their curse. Finding the gold is challeng-ing (difficulty) because it is hidden in a faraway island. But, it is not possible to obtain because they are able to discover where the gold is being stored. The crew buys-in to this goal (acceptance) because they believe that they will break their curse if the gold is found. And, finally, they know how well they are doing (feedback) based on how far they are away from the island and whether or not the curse is lifted.

The key here is that Barbossa knew that he cared about breaking the curse (i.e., he had this as a personal terminal value and goal) and it is aligned with the crews' goals because they also want to break the curse. He leveraged his instrumental values of obtaining his goal through whatever means possible. Because Barbossa's and his crew's goals agree, goal setting theory helps to explain why the crew is motivated to pursue Barbossa's desired end state that they share.

SUMMARY

In "Pirates of the Caribbean," just as in the real world, captains and leaders must make many decisions. The values and goals that are important to lead-ers should help guide their decisions, especially if they are aligned with those of their crew. This chapter considered the following:

- Leaders must engage in self-reflection to examine their own personal values and goals so that they come to understand what they truly care about.

- Once they are able to articulate their cares and desired end states, lead-ers should be purposeful in making decisions that are in line with their goals and values.

- If a leader's goals are aligned well with their followers, and the shared desired end states are clear, challenging, accepted by all, and allow for feedback, then followers will be motivated to accomplish them.

While following your personal compass ensures you stay true to your values, every ship still needs a captain to steer it through the storm. In the next chapter, we'll discuss the importance of decisive leadership and the challenges of being at the helm, proving that despite collaboration, there is only one captain.

8

THERE CAN ONLY BE ONE CAPTAIN

Taking audiences on a journey of adventure and intrigue on the high seas, the "Pirates of the Caribbean" series captivates audiences with tales of swashbuckling pirates, cursed treasures, and daring escapades. It goes beyond mere entertainment to offer profound insights into the intricate dynamics of leadership and management, from the cursed treasures of Isla de Muerta to the daring escapades aboard the Black Pearl. These tales offer valuable insights into management and leadership.

Having explored the vast waters of leadership in the Pirates of the Caribbean series, this chapter focuses on specific management principles that ensure crew success, whether at sea or in the boardroom. As we explore the actions and decisions of Captain Jack Sparrow, Captain Hector Barbossa, and their diverse crew, we gain a deeper understanding of fair compensation, effective problem-solving, and the balance between participatory and transformational leadership. Leaders can learn from these characters and their stories how to navigate challenges, foster loyalty, and lead their teams to shared success. Taking a fresh look at these familiar stories reveals valuable insights that continue to resonate in leadership and management today. In today's fast-paced business world, leaders and managers are becoming increasingly responsible for fostering a culture of trust and communication, being accountable and transparent, delegating not only tasks authority, empowering their team and last but not least addressing the issues early on before it gets too late manage them to create a more effective working environment. These competencies are necessary for current and future leaders to support their teams when they need it. As a leader, one of the most challenging tasks is ensuring that your team is free to act dynamically while maintaining control and avoiding mutiny. In the context of the "Pirates of the Caribbean" series, where mutinies are a common occurrence, this task becomes even more crucial. In the vast expanse of the high seas, where treachery and adventure collide, the "Pirates of the Caribbean" series offers a treasure trove of leadership lessons. No pearl of wisdom shines as brightly as the importance of fostering a culture of trust and communication, being accountable and transparent, delegating authority, and empowering your team. Here are some tips to help you ensure that your crew is free to act dynamically while also preventing mutinies.

NAVIGATING LEADERSHIP DYNAMICS

Establish Clear Leadership Roles

There is no doubt that the role of captain is well-defined and carries a great deal of responsibility in the world of pirates. In the "Pirates of the Caribbean" series, characters like Captain Jack Sparrow, Captain Hector Barbossa, and others understand the importance of establishing clear leadership roles. By defining and communicating these roles within their crews, they ensure smooth operations and maintain order.

For example, in "Pirates of the Caribbean: The Curse of the Black Pearl," the role of the captain is pivotal in the storyline. Captain Hector Barbossa establishes his leadership and authority over the Black Pearl crew. Despite his ruthless nature, Barbossa's role as captain is unmistakable, and his decisions are final. This clear leadership delineation prevents confusion and conflict among the crew. Everyone knows who holds ultimate authority, and this clarity helps maintain discipline and order on the ship.

Conversely, when Jack Sparrow becomes captain of the Black Pearl, his leadership style is more unconventional, yet he still establishes his role clearly. In "Pirates of the Caribbean: Dead Man's Chest," Jack's return as captain is met with various challenges, including a mutiny. However, by asserting his authority and making strategic decisions, such as negotiating with the East India Trading Company, he reestablishes his leadership. His crew obeys him whatever actions he takes, and his power as a captain is never questioned. According to French and Raven's framework of social power, leaders can use five bases of power to influence others: legitimate, reward, coercive, expert, and referent. Having legitimate power comes from a person's formal position or role within an organization, which grants them the authority to make decisions and expect compliance. A leader's reward power is based on their ability to provide incentives or rewards to others, such as promotions and raises. Having the ability to impose penalties or punishments for noncompliance gives you coercive power. Leaders' expertise or specialized knowledge gives them authority, which is respected by others. Lastly, referent power is derived from a leader's ability to attract admiration and loyalty based on their charisma or personal qualities (French & Raven, 1959).

Despite his erratic behavior, Jack's clear role as captain ensures that his crew understands who is in charge. This avoids power struggles and confusion. According to French and Raven's framework of social power, the title "captain" itself establishes Jack's legitimacy as a leader. Jack's legitimacy as captain of the Black Pearl can be attributed to his formal authority or position within a hierarchy. Even when Jack's actions are unpredictable or seem reckless, his crew is obliged to follow his decisions as a result of this formal recognition. Although the world of piracy is chaotic and uncertain, Jack benefits from his title as captain by maintaining order and leading his crew effectively.

Embrace Competence and Expertise

In the "Pirates of the Caribbean" series, the captain is not just a figurehead but someone who possesses the necessary skills, knowledge, and experience to lead. Captain Jack Sparrow's exceptional navigational abilities and strategic thinking make him a respected leader among his crew. As leaders, it is essential to continuously develop our competence and expertise in our respective fields. By demonstrating our skills and knowledge, we earn our team's trust and respect, making it easier to lead effectively. Jack's legitimate power as captain serves as the foundation upon which he builds additional forms of influence, he also has an expert power, derived from his vast knowledge of the sea and pirate lore, and referent power, derived from the loyalty and admiration he inspires among his crew.

For instance, in "Pirates of the Caribbean: Dead Man's Chest," Captain Jack Sparrow's competence is vividly demonstrated during the escape from the cannibal island. Faced with the daunting challenge of escaping captivity and outwitting the cannibals, Jack devises an ingenious plan involving make-shift cages and an elaborate ruse. His deep understanding of the environment and keen strategic mind enable him to lead his crew to safety. This episode showcases Jack's exceptional problem-solving skills and ability to navigate complex situations, reinforcing his credibility and authority as a leader.

Moreover, Jack's expertise in navigation and seamanship is evident throughout the series. In "Pirates of the Caribbean: The Curse of the Black Pearl," he masterfully pilots the Interceptor through a treacherous pursuit by the Black Pearl. His precise knowledge of the ship's capabilities and the surrounding waters allows him to make split-second decisions that keep his crew out of harm's way. This proficiency not only ensures the crew's safety but also cements Jack's status as a capable and trustworthy leader.

Balance Confidence and Humility

While there can only be one captain, effective leaders understand the importance of balancing confidence with humility. Captain Jack Sparrow exudes confidence in his abilities, but he also acknowledges his limitations and seeks help when needed. As leaders, it is crucial to have confidence in our decisions and actions but also to recognize that we are not infallible. Embracing humility allows us to learn from others, admit mistakes, and make better decisions for the team's benefit.

For instance, in "Pirates of the Caribbean: Dead Man's Chest," Captain Jack Sparrow's journey to find Davy Jones' heart exemplifies this balance. Jack is confident in his quest and ability to outmaneuver his enemies, yet he recognizes the need for allies and additional expertise. When Jack learns about Davy Jones' heart, he understands that he cannot retrieve it alone. He enlists the help of Will Turner and Elizabeth Swann, acknowledging that their skills and knowledge are crucial to the mission's success. Jack's willingness to seek assistance and value the contributions of others highlights his humility and understanding of his limitations.

Additionally, in "Pirates of the Caribbean: At World's End," Jack's humility is evident when he agrees to join forces with Captain Hector Barbossa despite their contentious history. Jack realizes that defeating the formidable East India Trading Company and freeing the goddess Calypso requires a united front. By setting aside his pride and collaborating with Barbossa, Jack demonstrates that true leadership involves recognizing others' strengths and leveraging them for the greater good. This collaboration ultimately leads to their victory and underscores the importance of humility in leadership.

Moreover, Jack's ability to admit mistakes and learn from them further illustrates his balanced approach. In "Pirates of the Caribbean: On Stranger Tides," Jack faces numerous challenges in his quest for the Fountain of Youth. When his plans turn out unsuccessful, he openly acknowledges his errors and adapts his strategies accordingly. This willingness to learn from setbacks and adjust his approach showcases Jack's humility and commitment to continuous improvement.

These examples from the "Pirates of the Caribbean" series illustrate that balancing confidence with humility is essential for effective leadership. Captain Jack Sparrow's ability to exude confidence while acknowledging his limitations and seeking help when needed makes him a relatable and respected leader. Similarly, in any leadership role, confidence in decisions and actions must be complemented by humility to learn from others, admit mistakes, and make better decisions for the team's benefit. Embracing this balance fosters a collaborative and adaptive leadership style that ultimately leads to greater success and stronger team dynamics.

Foster a Culture of Trust and Communication

Mutinies are one of the most serious threats to a captain's authority and crew cohesion in the world of piracy. Mutinies occur when crew members rebel against their captains and commanding officers, often because of grievances over poor conditions and leadership decisions. Mutinies have historically been a major concern not only on pirate ships but also on naval and merchant vessels, where power struggles, harsh conditions, and a lack of trust in leadership can lead to rebellion (Dancy, 2015).

There is a greater risk of mutinies in environments where communication is poor, trust has been eroded, and the crew feels that their concerns have not been addressed or heard. Leaders must understand the factors that lead to unrest if they wish to keep order.

Creating a culture of trust and communication among your crew is the first step toward preventing mutinies. Leaders can prevent opposition from turning into resistance by addressing concerns openly, ensuring fair treatment, and involving crew members in decision-making processes.

This means creating an environment where your crew feels comfortable expressing their concerns and ideas. In the second movie, when Elizabeth Swann questions Jack Sparrow's leadership, he responds that he is the only leader on the ship. Since Elizabeth is a pirate, just a part of the crew at this point in time in the films, she doesn't have any right to question his leadership. Thus because of her current rank, her ideas are not that important. In reality, most of the time leaders don't say this openly, but their behaviors unfortunately send a message to their team members that their ideas are not heard. Jack's attitude highlights the importance of creating an environment where all voices are heard and respected, regardless of rank.

An effective leadership culture is based on trust and open communication. In other movies in the "Pirate of the Caribbean" series, Captain Jack Sparrow exemplifies this principle and he shows that he can react differently to create a more loyal crew. In spite of Sparrow's enigmatic persona, his crew feels comfortable expressing their concerns and thoughts. His plans are shaped by taking into account their insights and ideas. As a result of nurturing open communication channels, Sparrow builds a crew that is loyal, nimble, and resilient.

There is a notable example of trust and communication in action when Captain Sparrow faces a mutiny aboard the Black Pearl. Instead of resorting to fear and intimidation, Sparrow addresses his crew's grievances through dialog and negotiation. As he acknowledges their concerns and involves them in decision-making, tension on board the ship is defused and harmony is restored. The actions of Sparrow demonstrate that trust and communication are essential elements of effective leadership, enabling leaders to successfully navigate even the stormiest of seas.

Be Accountable and Transparent

Maintaining order and morale in the unpredictable world of piracy requires accountability and transparency. This means explaining your reasoning and being open to feedback from your crew. Captain Hector Barbossa, a seasoned pirate who once commandeered the Black Pearl, understands this principle well. Barbossa does not shirk responsibility or hide behind excuses when faced with difficult decisions. Instead, he communicates openly with his crew and takes responsibility for his actions.

When Barbossa confronts the cursed treasure on Isla de Muerta, account-ability and transparency are evident. Instead of hoarding the cursed gold for himself, Barbossa intends to distribute it among his crew, ensuring they receive fair compensation. His open discussions of risks and rewards foster a sense of trust and unity among the crew. The actions of Barbossa demonstrate that true leadership requires honesty, integrity, and a responsibility to be accountable.

Delegate Authority and Empower Your Crew

To encourage dynamic action, delegating authority and empowering your crew to make decisions is essential. This means giving them the tools and resources they need to succeed and trusting them to act in the crew's best interests. In the third movie, when Will Turner is given the authority to lead a mission, he responds that if he does something to create an obstacle for their mission, the crew members have a right to correct his actions. This highlights the importance of empowering your crew to make decisions and take risks while holding them accountable for their actions.

Another great example of delegating authority and empowering other is the leadership of Elizabeth Swan, former captain of the Black Pearl, embodies this principle. Swann, despite her beginnings as a governor's daughter, proves herself a capable leader by delegating authority to her crew. Rather than micromanaging every detail of a daring raid against the East India Trading Company, Swann empowers her crew to make decisions and take action on their own initiative. When she trusts them and delegates authority to them, she unleashes their full potential and ensures their success. Swann demonstrates humility, trust, and a willingness to empower others through her actions as a leader.

To overcome adversity and achieve their goals, leaders must empower their crews. Captain Hector Barbossa, an experienced pirate who once sought the Fountain of Youth, understands this principle well. Barbossa empowers his crew to take ownership of their roles and responsibilities despite his tough exterior. Barbossa leads his crew on a quest to find the mystical Trident of Poseidon. Instead of dictating every aspect of their journey, Barbossa encourages his crew to share their ideas. He fosters a sense of pride and camaraderie among his crew by valuing their input and empowering them to take initiative. Barbossa's actions demonstrate the importance of trust, respect, and empowerment for true leadership. In "Pirates of the Caribbean: At World's End," Captain Hector Barbossa leads the crew of the Black Pearl on a dangerous journey to save Jack Sparrow from Davy Jones' Locker. As they navigate through the treacherous waters of the mysterious and dangerous sea, Barbossa consults with his crew, including Tia Dalma and others, about how to proceed. By listening to them, he demonstrates his leadership style that values trust, respect, and empowerment of his crew, which is essential for their survival and success.

Address Issues Early On

A leader's role is to prevent conflict from escalating and undermine the success of their endeavors at the earliest stage. The wily pirate, Jack Sparrow, who once sought the Dead Man's Chest, knows this. Sparrow recognizes the importance of nipping problems in the bud before they spiral out of control despite his penchant for mischief and mayhem. Sparrow discovers a plot to mutiny against him aboard the Black Pearl. He confronts the ringleaders and resolves the conflict through dialog and negotiation rather than waiting for the situation to worsen. By addressing the underlying grievances of his crew and seeking mutually beneficial solutions, he maintains their unity and cohesion. It takes vigilance, diplomacy, and a willingness to confront difficult issues for Sparrow to be an effective leader.

To prevent mutinies, addressing issues early on is crucial before they escalate. This translates to proactively identifying potential issues and taking steps to address them. In the franchise's fourth movie, when Captain Barbossa senses tension among his crew, he tries to solve this right away and openly points out the problem and says the crew can't create problems for other crew members. During "Pirates of the Caribbean: On Stranger Tides," Barbossa leads his crew on a quest for the Fountain of Youth as a privateer in service to the British crown.

After Barbossa and his crew have overcome various challenges, they arrive at the deserted Santiago, the ship of Ponce de León. They are tense as they face dangerous conditions, fear of Blackbeard, and general uncertainty of their mission. As Barbossa senses the unrest growing, he gathers his crew and speaks firmly about it. As he points out the problem, he emphasizes that any infighting or distractions will not be tolerated, emphasizing the importance of unity in order to succeed. They need to act as one team without conflicting to each other. Barbossa's words in that situation highlight the importance of awareness of potential conflicts and addressing them before they lead to mutinies.

Piracy is an unpredictable world, just like the real modern business world, that requires effective leadership in order to succeed and survive. By cultivating a culture of trust and communication, being accountable and transparent, delegating authority, empowering your crew, and addressing issues early on, leaders can navigate the treacherous waters of leadership with confidence and clarity. The "Pirates of the Caribbean" series teaches us that true leadership requires humility, integrity, and a willingness to empower others. Ensuring that your team is free to act dynamically while maintaining control requires a delicate balance of trust, accountability, delegation, and proactive problem-solving.

Respect and Adapt to Change

The "Pirates of the Caribbean" characters often find themselves in unpredictable and challenging situations. Effective leaders understand the need to adapt to change and make quick decisions when circumstances demand them. Captain Jack Sparrow's ability to think on his feet and adapt to unexpected challenges showcases leadership flexibility and resilience. By embracing change and encouraging a culture of adaptability, leaders can navigate uncertain waters and steer their teams toward success.

For example, in "Pirates of the Caribbean: The Curse of the Black Pearl," Captain Jack Sparrow faces numerous unpredictable challenges as he seeks to reclaim his ship, the Black Pearl. One of the most notable instances is when he and Will Turner infiltrate Port Royal to rescue Elizabeth Swann. The situation quickly escalates, and Jack has to adapt his plans on the fly. This example highlights Jack's capacity to respect and adapt to change, an essential quality of effective leadership. His quick thinking and ability to improvise under pressure enable him to navigate through chaos and ultimately achieve his objectives. In "Pirates of the Caribbean: The Curse of the Black Pearl," Jack is captured by the British Navy in Port Royal. By improvising a daring escape, he uses the ropes and pulleys he finds to swing around, fighting off guards, and ultimately escaping from the gallows. Despite a seemingly hopeless situation, Jack was able to adapt to the situation, use the environment to his advantage, and think several steps ahead of his pursuers. He often succeeds in achieving his objectives despite overwhelming odds thanks to cleverness, resourcefulness, and luck.

Likewise, in "Pirates of the Caribbean: Dead Man's Chest," Jack is confronted with the imminent threat of Davy Jones and his monstrous Kraken. Initially, Jack tries to evade danger, but when it becomes inevitable, he shifts his strategy and seeks to find Davy Jones' heart to gain leverage over him. This scenario demonstrates Jack's resilience and adaptability in the face of unforeseen threats. His willingness to alter his approach and make swift decisions in response to changing circumstances underscores leadership flexibility.

Furthermore, in "Pirates of the Caribbean: At World's End," the alliance between some pirates and the East India Trading Company creates a complex and volatile environment. Captain Jack Sparrow, along with other pirate leaders that aren't aligned with the East Inda Trading Company, must navigate this treacherous landscape. Jack's ability to form alliances, renegotiate terms, and adapt to shifting loyalties proves crucial in their efforts to combat a common enemy. This adaptability not only helps Jack survive but also enables him to turn potential adversaries (i.e., the other Pirate Lords) into allies. This demonstrates the power of flexible leadership in dynamic situations.

Another compelling example is found in "Pirates of the Caribbean: On Stranger Tides." Here, Jack embarks on a quest to find the Fountain of Youth, facing numerous unexpected challenges along the way. From dealing with Blackbeard's unpredictable wrath to navigating treacherous mermaid-infested waters, Jack consistently adapts to every challenge with ingenuity and resilience. His ability to remain flexible and resourceful in the face of constant change allows him to guide his crew through perilous situations, ultimately steering them toward their goal. The monstrous Kraken chases Jack in "Pirates of the Caribbean: Dead Man's Chest." As the beast repeatedly attacks the Black Pearl, Jack realizes that conventional fighting methods will not work. To create a diversion, he orders the crew to abandon the ship instead of attacking the Kraken directly. Jack then returns to the ship with his iconic compass and sword to face the Kraken, buying time for his crew to escape.

These examples from the Pirates of the Caribbean series illustrate the critical importance of respecting and adapting to changes in leadership. Captain

Jack Sparrow's capacity to think on his feet and respond to unpredictable challenges highlights the necessity of flexibility and resilience. By embracing change and fostering a culture of adaptability, leaders can effectively navigate uncertain situations and guide their teams toward success. This approach not only enhances the leader's ability to manage crises but also empowers the team to thrive in a constantly evolving environment.

EMBRACE DIVERSE IDEAS

Effective managers recognize the value of diverse perspectives and encourage their team members to contribute their unique ideas. Jack Sparrow, across the deck of the Black Pearl, reminds his crew that success lay in embracing different viewpoints and thinking outside the box.

Captain Sparrow exemplifies inclusive leadership by valuing the skills and expertise of each member of his ship. He knows that the strength of his crew lies in their diversity – a blend of sailors from different backgrounds, cultures, and experiences. From the skilled navigator who have once sailed with the East India Trading Company to the resourceful shipwright who have learned his craft in a distant port, the captain recognized the potential in every individual. Every member of the crew, whether it was Mr. Gibbs, a skilled navigator who once sailed with the East India Trading Company, or another resourceful crew member who brought a unique talent to the ship, the captain recognized their potential.

Inclusive leadership, like the "Pirates of the Caribbean" series itself, emphasizes the power of unity amidst diversity. By embracing diverse ideas and encouraging team members to contribute their unique insights, leaders can unlock the true potential of their teams.

In Captain Sparrow's world, diversity wasn't just about race or gender but also about recognizing the distinct strengths and talents that individuals brought to the table (Kuknor & Bhattacharya, 2022).

Just as Captain Sparrow navigated through treacherous waters, inclusive leaders navigate complex challenges, drawing on the collective wisdom of their team. They understand that diversity isn't a liability to be managed but an asset to be celebrated. Inclusive leaders create a breeding ground for innovation, creativity, and better decision-making by fostering an environment where different viewpoints are respected and welcomed.

The crew of the Black Pearl, each with their quirks and eccentricities, united under the leadership of Captain Jack Sparrow. They thrived because they felt valued, heard, and included. And in their journey to conquer the unknown, they discovered that the strength of their diverse crew lay not just in their differences but also in their shared purpose and camaraderie.

As leaders set sail on their personal journeys, they must remember the lessons of Captain Sparrow and the "Pirates of the Caribbean" – that by embracing diverse ideas, fostering inclusive environments, and valuing the perspectives of all, they can chart a course to success that is as captivating and exhilarating as a pirate's life on the high seas.

In addition to the good side of leadership, "Pirates of the Caribbean" characters also show us examples of ineffective and unethical leadership practices. When leaders are ineffective, they fail to create change due to missing traits, weak skills, poor strategies, and unethical leadership without a sense of right and wrong (Kellerman, 2004). Although these characters may achieve short-term success, they often show critical pitfalls that leaders should avoid in real life.

Unethical Leadership: The Path to Downfall

An important lesson from the series is the danger of unethical leadership. Some characters in the Pirates of the Caribbean films engage in corrupt practices to maintain their power, only to be brought to their knees by their own actions.

The "Curse of the Black Pearl," for instance, shows Captain Barbossa disregarding ethical leadership. He betrays his crew, violates the Pirate Code, and rules through fear and intimidation. Although Barbossa initially succeeds in achieving his goals, his unethical behavior leads to rebellion and mistrust among his followers, demonstrating that unethical leadership is unsustainable (Brown & Treviño, 2006).

Similarly, Captain Davy Jones in "Dead Man's Chest" exemplifies a leader who uses cruelty and manipulation to maintain control. Rather than respecting his crew, he punishes them severely and exploits their weaknesses to ensure obedience. Negative leadership practices may be successful in the short term but ultimately fail and lead to loyalty loss.

The Dangers of Leader Isolation

Another leadership pitfall is isolation of leaders. This occurs when leaders become disconnected from their followers, resulting in poor decision-making and a breakdown in trust and communication.

The dangers of leader isolation are reflected in Captain Barbossa's obsession with the Fountain of Youth in On Stranger Tides. As a result of his single-minded pursuit of his goal, he neglects the needs and concerns of his crew, resulting in mutiny. This example underscores how isolation can erode trust and support, rendering leadership ineffective (Riggio, 2015).

Charismatic Leadership: A Double-edged Sword

Additionally, the series explores the challenges of charismatic leadership. While charisma can inspire and motivate, it can also lead to manipulation and a lack of accountability.

Captain Jack Sparrow's leadership style is a prime example of this. In "The Curse of the Black Pearl," Jack uses his charm and wit to manipulate Will Turner and gain his crew's trust. As a result of his self-serving actions, several crew members died and his promises were not fulfilled. As a result of his passion for personal gain, Jack's charismatic leadership is undermined, resulting in a breakdown of trust between him and his followers (Conger & Kanungo, 1987; House, 1976).

Similarly, Captain Barbossa's charismatic persona initially attracts loyalty, but his lack of emotional connection and accountability with his crew eventually leads to his downfall. His leadership style, while effective in the short term, ultimately proves unsustainable because it is not grounded in genuine concern for his followers.

This series teaches us that sometimes it is better to have only one captain to lead effectively. One strong leader, however, can also bring out the dark side of leadership that is ineffective and unethical. From unethical practices to charismatic leadership, characters in the "Pirates of the Caribbean" demonstrate the importance of ethical behavior, maintaining a connection with followers, and balancing charisma with accountability. Leaders and managers can gain valuable insight from these portrayals and avoid these critical "don'ts" in their leadership approaches (Brown & Treviño, 2006; Conger & Kanungo, 1987; House, 1976; Patterson, 2003; Riggio, 2015).

SUMMARY

In this chapter, we discussed how leaders can navigate difficult challenges with humility, integrity, and a commitment to empowering their teams by learning from the mistakes and successes of "Pirates of the Caribbean" characters. Leadership success will come from embracing diverse ideas, fostering inclusive environments, and valuing all perspectives.

We considered the following:

- Leaders must address difficult issues to maintain unity and cohesion among their team.

- Leaders should create a culture where all voices are heard and respected to foster culture and communication.

- Leaders unleash their team's full potential and ensure success, by delegating authority and empowering their team.

- While charismatic leaders can inspire loyalty, they may also prioritize personal agendas over organizational needs.

We must recognize that true leadership thrives when everyone on board feels valued once we've navigated the challenges of being the captain. The next chapter, "Part of the Crew, Part of the Ship," will discuss how you can transform a solitary captain's journey into a unified voyage of shared success by cultivating a sense of belonging among your crew.

9

PART OF THE CREW, PART OF THE SHIP

Leadership requires more than authority and discipline to maintain a motivated and dedicated team; it requires fair compensation as well. Whether it is tangible rewards, opportunities for growth, or recognition, effective leaders recognize that their team's loyalty and commitment depend on feeling adequately rewarded. Leaders can maintain a harmonious and productive work environment by ensuring team members feel valued and fairly treated.

In this chapter, we examine the alignment between fair compensation principles and equity theory in management. By examining Barbossa's leadership decisions, we draw parallels to real-world leadership challenges, exploring how fair compensation can serve as a powerful tool for preventing discontent and fostering a motivated, dedicated team. It is important to balance rewards and maintain team morale when dealing with the complexities of leadership within any organization.

FAIR COMPENSATION

To keep their crew motivated and dedicated, managers must ensure fair compensation. The infamous conversation between Captain Barbossa and Elizabeth Swann comes to mind. Elizabeth and Barbossa's conversations about rules and bending rules remind us that while pirates might bend the rules, a good manager should ensure fair compensation to retain talent and prevent grievances from brewing on their own ship.

As a captain, Barbossa understands the importance of fair compensation in maintaining the loyalty of his crew by bending the rules when necessary.

When it comes to making decisions for the survival and success of his crew, Barbossa often operates within a moral gray area. Despite not always following traditional codes of honor, he ensures that his crew is adequately compensated, whether through treasure, freedom, or breaking curses.

Barbossa and his men become immortal after stealing the cursed gold in "Pirates of the Caribbean: The Curse of the Black Pearl." However, they are unable to feel any physical sensations. They must return all the stolen gold and repay it with blood in order to break the curse. While Barbossa knows Elizabeth Swann isn't the rightful owner of the blood required to lift the curse, he deceives her into believing she is the last piece needed.

Captain Barbossa understood the importance of fair compensation in maintaining the loyalty and dedication of his crew. He knew that a disgruntled sailor could easily become a mutinous one. With the vast treasure chests acquired during their plundering escapades, Barbossa ensured his crew received their fair share.

Captain Barbossa, embracing the principles of equity theory, understood that his crew compared their inputs and outputs to those of their peers. It wasn't just about dividing the treasure equally but recognizing and acknowledging individual efforts and contributions. By ensuring fair compensation, Barbossa prevented feelings of inequity from taking root and mutinous attitudes from festering among his crew (Al-Zawahreh & Al-Madi, 2012).

EQUITY THEORY

Equity theory, in the "Pirates of the Caribbean" context, unveils a crucial lesson for managers: fairness in compensation is paramount. Like a pirate crew, employees in any organization compare their efforts and skills to those of their colleagues. When individuals perceive an imbalance between their inputs and outputs, feelings of inequity arise, leading to demotivation and even rebellion.

By upholding fair compensation practices, managers can create a sense of justice and maintain the motivation of their crew, just as Captain Barbossa did with his pirate band. It is not merely about the financial rewards but also about recognizing one's contributions and the sense of being valued. When employees perceive that their efforts are fairly rewarded, they are more likely to remain committed, engaged, and willing to go the extra nautical mile.

In real life, when the managers navigate the choppy waters of leadership, they should remember the wisdom of Captain Barbossa and the "Pirates of the Caribbean" – that fair compensation is not just a guideline but a compass that steers the ship toward a harmonious and productive crew. Although Barbossa does not explicitly emphasize the importance of fair compensation in the traditional sense, he does demonstrate a keen sense of maintaining loyalty and avoiding mutiny by balancing the interests of his crew. In "Pirates of the Caribbean: The Curse of the Black Pearl," Barbossa ensures that his crew members are motivated by the promise of breaking the curse and regaining their ability to feel physical pleasure, which can be perceived as compensation.

Barbossa's leadership often relies on ensuring that his crew believes, regardless of whether they're seeking gold, freedom, or breaking a curse, that they'll get what they want. The understanding of what motivates his crew can be compared with the concept of fair compensation in real-life leadership, where managers must ensure their teams feel valued and adequately rewarded.

By recognizing the inputs and outputs of their team members and ensuring a sense of equity, managers can prevent mutinous attitudes and cultivate an environment where everyone feels valued and motivated to sail toward shared success. For managers to effectively apply equity theory, they must focus on both the inputs and outputs of their employees. Inputs include employee effort, skills, time, and loyalty, while outputs refer to the rewards they receive in return, such as salary, recognition, promotions, and other benefits (Adams, 1965). Employees feel motivated and valued when their input is fairly rewarded, reducing the likelihood of dissatisfaction or "mutinous attitudes" in the workplace. Employees who perceive inequity may adapt their efforts or seek fairness through other means as a result of reduced motivation and morale.

Maintaining a balance between inputs and outputs is crucial for motivating and engaging employees. By ensuring that rewards are perceived as fair, recognizing contributions appropriately, and maintaining open communication, managers can prevent discontent.

EFFECTIVE PROBLEM-SOLVING

Managers should empower their crew to solve problems effectively. In the midst of a perilous escape from the clutches of the East India Trading

Company, Captain Jack Sparrow found himself cornered, surrounded by enemies on all sides. Yet, during his different adventures with his crew, Jack with a mischievous smile and a glint in his eye, he calmly declares they would go after a something valuable to motivate his crew. Jack Sparrow's words ignited a spark of resourcefulness and creativity within his crew, reminding them there is always a way forward, even in the face of adversity, and a reward awaits them.

Captain Sparrow embodied the essence of design thinking, a management approach that promotes a collaborative and iterative process for problem-solving. He understood that to overcome challenges, they needed to adopt a mindset that focused not on the problem itself but on finding innovative solutions. Design thinking urged them to dive deep into understanding user needs, generate a plethora of ideas, prototype potential solutions, and test them to ensure effectiveness.

Amidst the swirling mists of a hidden island, Captain Sparrow led his crew through a design-thinking journey. They huddled together, discussing the intricacies of their predicament and considering various perspectives to plan important battles. These discussions often involved brainstorming and evaluating different approaches to overcome the challenges they faced, demonstrating a collaborative approach to problem-solving.

Design thinking allowed them to explore unconventional paths and stretch the limits of their imagination. With every challenge they encountered, they delved into the depths of creativity and resourcefulness, searching for that one breakthrough idea that could turn the tide in their favor. They built prototypes of their plans, testing them against the harsh realities of the pirate's life and refining them until they discovered the perfect blend of audacity and feasibility (Micheli et al., 2019).

Design thinking transcends conventional problem-solving in the world of "Pirates of the Caribbean." It embodies the spirit of adventure, curiosity, and innovation. It fuels a dynamic and inclusive environment where every idea is valued, and creativity knows no bounds. By embracing design thinking, managers empower their crew to think beyond the obvious, challenge the status quo, and discover unconventional yet effective solutions.

By adopting a design thinking mindset, managers can unlock the treasure trove of their team's creativity, navigate through storms of uncertainty, and find solutions that not only solve the problem at hand but also propel their organization toward new horizons of success.

A good manager must create an environment where mutinous behaviors are minimized. Captain Barbossa understood that preventing mutinies required more than just fear and discipline. It demanded a leadership style that fostered a sense of ownership and involvement among the crew. Participative leadership, a theory that resonates with the ethos of the "Pirates of the Caribbean," became the guiding compass for Barbossa as he navigated the treacherous waters of management.

Captain Barbossa gathered his crew in the heart of a stormy night as waves crashed against the ship's bow. The rum-soaked air carried whispers of dissent and the potential for mutiny. With a commanding presence, Barbossa invited his crew to participate in decision-making processes. He knew that the likelihood of mutinous behavior decreased when everyone felt heard and valued. Barbossa is a strong, authoritative leader who often makes decisions on his own or with other leaders, rather than through open discussion with the entire crew. In "At World's End," his leadership evolves as he takes on more responsibility and faces challenges that require alliances.

Through participative leadership, Barbossa encouraged his crew to voice their opinions, share their concerns, and contribute ideas. In the dimly lit quarters, debates roared like a storm. The seasoned quartermaster argued for one course of action, while the cunning first mate proposed an alternative approach. Barbossa listened attentively to each voice, considering the insights of his crew before charting the ship's course. Various pirate lords, including Barbossa, debate on the best strategy against their enemies in "Pirates of the Caribbean: At World's End." Before making strategic decisions, Barbossa listens to the different opinions of his crew and takes the lead when needed.

Participative leadership extends beyond strategic decisions. It encompassed the day-to-day life of the crew, involving them in the allocation of tasks, the division of responsibilities, and even the rules that governed their pirate code. Barbossa ensured that each member had a sense of ownership and responsibility through this inclusive approach, reducing resistance to change and mutinous tendencies (Wang et al., 2022).

As they embarked on their search for the fabled Fountain of Youth, Captain Barbossa's participative leadership style continued to prove its worth. Crew members felt a genuine sense of belonging, and their loyalty to the captain grew stronger with every passing day. They understood that their contributions mattered, that their voices were heard, and that they could overcome any challenge the sea presented together. During the battle against the cursed pirates in "Pirates of the Caribbean: The Curse of the Black Pearl," there is a sense of belonging and loyalty among the crew. Despite their differences and the risks involved, the crew members stand by Jack, trusting in his leadership and believing in their collective strength to succeed. Their willingness to fight alongside him proves the strong bonds and mutual respect they have developed, making them a strong team.

Participative leadership transcends traditional management practices within the world of Pirates of the Caribbean. It forges bonds of trust and camaraderie, instilling a sense of unity that surpasses the shackles of rank or hierarchy.

By involving employees in decision-making processes and enhancing their sense of ownership, participative leaders create a crew that is not just a group of individuals but a tightly knit family united by a common purpose.

By embracing participative leadership, managers can create an environment where every voice is valued, every idea is considered, and mutinous behavior gives way to a crew that is loyal, dedicated, and prepared to face any challenge that comes their way on the vast expanse of the open sea.

EFFECTIVE COMMUNICATION

Clear and effective communication is vital for a successful crew. Will Turner is often transparent and honest. In his efforts to save his father and protect those he cares about, he consistently acts with integrity, making his intentions clear and being transparent about his goals. Will's straightforward nature helps to build trust with those around him. Will Turner's leadership highlights the importance of transparency and honesty to build trust and foster effective communication channels.

Captain Sparrow, despite his eccentricities, recognized the importance of transformational leadership in creating a cohesive and motivated crew. Transformational leaders possess the ability to inspire and motivate their teams through effective communication, building trust, and creating a shared vision. They go beyond simply giving orders and inspire their crew to reach greater heights.

On the deck of the Black Pearl, Captain Sparrow would gather his crew and cast a vision of grandeur. With his unmistakable charm, he painted a picture of untold riches and the thrill of adventure that awaited them on their journey. His words, laced with conviction and charisma, ignited a fire within his crew, filling their hearts with a sense of purpose and a shared sense of destiny.

Transformational leaders understand that effective communication is the lifeblood of their crew. They establish open channels where ideas flow freely, and feedback is welcomed. Captain Sparrow, known for his enigmatic personality, fostered an environment where his crew felt comfortable expressing their thoughts and concerns. He listened intently to their insights, incorporating their ideas into the fabric of their plans (Montuori & Donnelly, 2018). In "Pirates of the Caribbean: The Curse of the Black Pearl," Jack consults Mr. Gibbs and others about outmaneuvers their opponents. Jack often makes the final decisions, but he values the input of his crew and incorporates their ideas into his plans, demonstrating his leadership style of balancing authority with collaboration.

With each daring escapade, the crew of the Black Pearl encountered unexpected challenges. Yet, under the leadership of Captain Sparrow, they navigated through treacherous waters with unwavering determination. When storms threatened to engulf them, Sparrow rallied his crew with words of encouragement and resilience. He highlighted how his team stronger than any problems they would face including the dealing with a rough sea and his voice was carrying the conviction of a truly transformational leader.

In "Pirates of the Caribbean," transformational leadership becomes the compass that guides the ship through uncharted waters. It is more than just a management style; it inspires individuals to transcend their limitations and embrace their full potential.

By establishing effective communication channels, building trust, and creating a shared vision, transformational leaders create an environment where crew members become empowered, motivated, and driven to achieve greatness.

The "Pirates of the Caribbean" series provides a captivating and engaging perspective on how these management theories can be applied in real-world scenarios by embracing diverse ideas, ensuring fair compensation, problem-solving effectively, minimizing mutinies, and participatory leadership to transformational leadership.

All these perspectives are valuable insights into various management theories that can be applied in the real world. From the importance of embracing diverse ideas to ensuring fair compensation, from adopting a solution-oriented mindset to involving the crew in decision-making processes, and from mini-mizing mutinies through participative leadership to inspiring and motivating through effective communication, the leadership lessons from the high seas can inspire managers to become more effective leaders in their domains.

It is important to accept diversity, foster inclusiveness, and create environments where all voices are heard and valued. A leader who successfully navigates complex challenges must draw on the collective wisdom and diverse perspectives of their team, as Captain Jack Sparrow does in treacherous waters. Leaders can unlock their teams' maximum potential and steer them toward shared success by encouraging them to solve problems creatively and involve them in decision-making processes. In order to achieve organizational goals, leaders can cultivate loyal, dedicated, and motivated crews through fair compensation practices, participatory leadership, and effective communication. As a timeless compass, the leadership lessons from the "Pirates of the Caribbean" series help managers become more effective leaders in their domains and inspire them to chart their own course toward greatness.

SUMMARY

This chapter explored how diverse perspectives are valuable to effective leaders, and team members should be encouraged to contribute their unique perspectives. Innovative solutions are produced when leaders embrace each individual's strengths and differences. By drawing on the collective wisdom of their diverse team, leaders can navigate challenges more effectively by instilling a sense of belonging among team members. Ultimately, leaders can unlock the true potential of their teams by embracing diversity and encouraging all team members to contribute.

We considered the following:

- An effective leader encourages team members to contribute unique ideas and embraces the perspectives of others. Leaders who recognize individual strengths and celebrate diversity can unlock the true potential of their teams and navigate challenges more effectively.

- Through inclusive leadership, different viewpoints are protected and respected, and innovation, creativity, and better decision-making are encouraged.

- Leaders must ensure fair compensation to keep their team motivated and dedicated. Providing fair compensation goes beyond financial rewards to recognize one's contributions and foster a sense of value and motivation.

- The design thinking process promotes unconventional path-finding, encourages creativity, and helps organizations achieve success.

- Leaders who adopt a design thinking mindset can unlock their team's creativity, navigate uncertainty, and find effective solutions to complex issues.

- A participative leadership style builds trust and camaraderie within a company, transcending traditional management practices.

- When leaders involve employees in decision-making processes and enhance their sense of ownership, mutinous behavior can be avoided, and unified, motivated teams can emerge.

The ship sails smoothly when every crew member plays their part, and a sense of unity is visible. We will explore the complexity of risk management in the next chapter, examining how effective leadership can drive organization-wide transformations and turn challenges into opportunities

10

TIDES OF CHANGE

Risk management plays a key role in the sustainability, stability, and success of any organization. In a constantly changing environment, leaders must navigate risks posed by market fluctuations, regulatory changes, technological advancements, and operational inefficiencies. It is essential to recognize and manage these risks as a proactive approach to seizing opportunities and achieving long-term goals.

Using the "Pirates of the Caribbean" movie series as inspiration, we can gain a unique insight into risk management. During their adventures, Captain Jack Sparrow faces numerous hazards, from cursed pirates to treacherous waters. Leadership lessons can be learned from their ability to assess risks, make quick decisions, and adapt to changing circumstances.

We will examine why effective risk management is crucial for leaders. We will also discuss the multifaceted role of risk management, emphasizing its importance in protecting organizational assets and reputation, ensuring compliance and legal protection, facilitating decision-making, cultivating a culture of resilience and agility, supporting innovation and growth, fostering trust and confidence, and ensuring long-term success. In examining these aspects and drawing parallels with Captain Jack Sparrow's adventures, we aim to provide a comprehensive understanding of how leaders can use risk management to steer their organizations toward success.

SYSTEMS THEORY

Systems theory sees organizations as interconnected and interdependent systems. In risk management, this perspective emphasizes the need to understand how different areas of an organization interact and how risks can affect them all. It suggests analyzing an organization as a whole, considering the interactions and relationships between its various components. As a result of this holistic approach, it is possible to identify how risks from one department or process may ripple out and affect other areas.

Systems thinking can help leaders identify systemic risks and develop comprehensive strategies that consider the interconnectedness of different organizational components (von Bertalanffy, 2015). Supply chain disruptions, for example, may affect more than just production. They may also impact sales, customer satisfaction, and financial stability. Leaders can implement more effective risk mitigation strategies by understanding these connections.

Risk Management in Systems Theory

As the Pirates of the Caribbean navigate uncertainty and ensure success, the concept of a risk management model emerges as critical. In this model, potential threats to a pirate crew's mission, such as rival attacks, mutinies, and treacherous waters, are identified and documented. The use of brainstorming techniques among crew members, historical logs, and SWOT analysis (strengths, weaknesses, opportunities, and threats) all play important roles (Hopkin & Thompson, 2021). In the next phase, risk assessment, these risks are evaluated based on their likelihood and potential impact. To assess the severity and probability of threats, qualitative methods like risk matrices and expert judgment from seasoned sailors, along with quantitative techniques like probability and impact analysis, are used.

Understanding Interdependencies

"Pirates of the Caribbean" demonstrates the interconnectedness of risks. The actions of each character in "Dead Man's Chest" affect the outcomes for everyone involved, whether it's Jack Sparrow, Will Turner, or Davy Jones. To escape his debt to Davy Jones, which puts him at odds with Will Turner, who also fights with Jones. Davy Jones, in turn, seeks to maintain his power and avoid vulnerability. There is a ripple effect between each character's actions, such that decisions made by one character affect those of the others, underscoring their interdependence. Likewise, leaders must understand how risks in one part of their organization can affect others.

Identifying Systemic Risks

The curse of the Black Pearl impacts every member of the crew in the first film of the series, so systemic risks in an organization can affect everyone. "The Curse of the Black Pearl" impacts every crew member by turning them into undead beings, unable to feel or experience life fully. Their existence is tortured by a curse that strips them of their basic human senses, such as taste and touch. Every crew member is equally affected by the curse, demonstrating how systemic risks can affect everyone in an organization. Leaders must analyze how different components of the organization interact to identify these risks.

Developing Comprehensive Strategies

"At World's End" illustrates the necessity of a coordinated approach to managing threats through the combined efforts of various pirate factions. Similarly, in risk management, developing strategies that consider the entire system ensures that risk mitigation is not siloed but integrated across the organization. In order to accomplish this, departments and stakeholders might need to collaborate on coordinated risk management plans.

By incorporating systems theory into risk management, leaders can view their organizations holistically and understand how interdependencies can impact the risks they face. In order to develop effective risk mitigation strategies, leaders must recognize how different parts of the organization are interconnected. This will ensure that risks are managed holistically and integrated. As a result of this approach, the organization's resilience and ability to adapt to changing conditions is enhanced, and risk is identified and addressed more effectively. Leaders can, therefore, fulfill their leadership responsibilities, develop organizational strategies, and improve their organizations through risk management.

Protecting Organizational Assets and Reputation

A leader's responsibility is to keep the organization's finances in good shape and create a positive reputation for it. Risk management helps leaders identify potential financial threats, such as market fluctuations, credit risks, and operational inefficiencies, and take proactive measures to mitigate them. Risk management allows leaders to prevent incidents that could damage their organization's reputation, such as data breaches, compliance failures, or unethical behavior. Throughout the series, Jack Sparrow and his crew continually manage the risks of losing their ship, the Black Pearl, which is central to their identity and success. They take calculated actions to protect it from enemies and threats.

Enhancing Decision-making

Leaders can make well-informed decisions based on comprehensive insights into potential threats and opportunities provided by risk management. This includes strategic planning, resource allocation, and investment decisions. Leaders can gain a competitive edge by understanding and managing risks. As a result, they may be able to take calculated risks that competitors may not take, potentially leading to greater innovation and market leadership. When it serves a greater purpose, Jack forms temporary alliances with rivals when it balances risk and reward.

Fostering a Culture of Resilience and Agility

Organizational resilience can be built through effective risk management. In the event of a crisis, leaders can prepare their teams to respond effectively, ensuring continuity of operations while minimizing disruption. Business environments are constantly changing, so leaders need to be flexible. Through risk management, leaders can anticipate and respond quickly to emerging threats and opportunities, keeping the organization agile and flexible. Jack and his crew's adaptability is evident in their ability to handle unpredictable situations, such as sudden changes in battle tides or unexpected betrayals.

Building Trust and Confidence

Risk management builds trust among stakeholders, including employees, investors, customers, and partners. A proactive approach to managing risks is more likely to be supported by stakeholders. A company that prioritizes risk management makes employees feel safer and more confident. As a result, morale can be raised, engagement can be increased, and performance can be improved.

Risk management is integral to effective leadership. Leaders can use it to protect their organizations, make informed decisions, cultivate a culture of resilience, and build trust among their employees. Managing risk allows leaders to navigate uncertainty with confidence, seize opportunities, and guide their organizations toward sustainable growth and prosperity. Jack Sparrow's leadership, despite its flaws, often cultivates loyalty and confidence in his crew through his ability to steer them through dangers.

ESSENTIAL LEADERSHIP SKILLS FOR EFFECTIVE RISK MANAGEMENT

Leaders need a wide range of skills, so they can effectively manage risks. Captain Jack Sparrow and his crew embody these essential skills on their exciting journeys. Captain Jack Sparrow and his crew demonstrate key risk management skills throughout their adventures. As a result of Sparrow's strong situational awareness and flexibility, he can adapt to changing situations on the fly and manage risks effectively. It is also important for the crew to work together and communicate, as they often rely on each other's expertise to navigate dangers. Additionally, Sparrow's strategic thinking, such as forming alliances and anticipating opponents' moves, demonstrates his foresight and planning skills, which are essential for reducing risk.

Analytical Thinking: Problem Identification and Information Analysis

Observation and analysis help Jack Sparrow identify the curse affecting the crew of the Black Pearl in "The Curse of the Black Pearl." Similarly, leaders need to analyze data and trends to identify potential risks. In "Dead Man's Chest," Jack interprets complex clues leading to Davy Jones' heart, understanding potential outcomes and risks. Understanding the likelihood and impact of different risks requires leaders to analyze complex data.

Decision-making: Risk Assessment and Strategic Choices

Jack assesses the risks and decides how to proceed before venturing into dangerous waters. Leaders need to evaluate the potential consequences of different risks and make informed decisions about how to mitigate them. As a result of Jack's strategic thinking, he aligned himself with unlikely partners in order to achieve his goals. Leaders need to balance risk and reward when making strategic decisions, taking both short- and long-term perspectives into account.

In "The Curse of the Black Pearl," Jack Sparrow and Will Turner need a fast ship to catch up with the Black Pearl. The crew decides to steal the fastest ship in the Caribbean. Jack assesses the risks of stealing a ship from their powerful enemy, including the potential for capture and execution. As a result of evaluating the strengths and weaknesses of the ship, he determines that it is the best option for their mission. Even though the risks are high, Jack decides that the ship's speed and capabilities outweigh the risks. A thorough assessment is essential when weighing potential rewards against risks and making strategic decisions.

In "Dead Man's Chest," Jack Sparrow is in need of allies to escape Davy Jones and the Kraken. It is not uncommon for him to form alliances with unlikely partners, including former rivals and enemies. When evaluating the risks of aligning with characters like Elizabeth Swann and James Norrington, Jack takes into account their past conflicts and differing goals. In addition, he assesses Davy Jones's risks and the necessity of a united front in order to survive. By aligning with these unlikely partners, Jack seeks to strengthen their collective strength against a common enemy. To achieve long-term goals, strategic alliances and the ability to see past immediate differences are essential.

In "On Stranger Tides," Jack Sparrow embarks on a perilous quest to find an important target. In addition to the threat from Blackbeard and the Spanish Armada, Jack carefully assesses the risks associated with the journey. His focus is on the potential rewards of finding the Fountain and the challenges he will face along the way. Jack's decision to pursue the Fountain of Youth, despite its risks, is driven by his strategic vision of achieving immortality and gaining a powerful advantage. It is important to balance short-term risks with long-term rewards when making strategic decisions.

Jack Sparrow must navigate Calypso's maelstrom in order to confront his enemies and achieve his goals during "At World's End." He assesses the risks of battle inside the maelstrom, including the unpredictable nature of the storm and the formidable forces against him. He evaluates the strategic advantages as well as the potential pitfalls of fighting under such treacherous conditions. Jack decides to engage in the battle, using the chaos of the maelstrom to his advantage. By leveraging environmental factors and making strategic choices, potential disadvantages can be turned into opportunities.

Leaders can gain a better understanding of risk assessment and strategic thinking by studying Jack Sparrow's decision-making processes in "Pirates of the Caribbean." Developing these skills is essential to navigating the complexities of modern leadership and making successful decisions.

Communication: Persuasion and Negotiation

Throughout the voyage, Jack communicates his plans effectively to his crew, ensuring that everyone is clear about their roles. Leaders must communicate risk-related information clearly to stakeholders, including team members, executives, and external partners. Jack demonstrated his persuasive skills during his negotiations with Barbossa and other pirates. It is the leaders' responsibility to convince stakeholders that risk management measures are important and to negotiate solutions to mitigate risks.

In "The Curse of the Black Pearl," Jack Sparrow battles Captain Hector Barbossa, who has taken control of the Black Pearl and is trying to break a curse. As an opportunist, Jack must negotiate with Barbossa to achieve his goals. Jack convinces Barbossa to form an uneasy alliance using his persuasive skills. Despite their history of betrayal and mutual distrust, Jack convinces Barbossa that they share a common enemy. Jack successfully negotiates terms that serve his interests, including gaining temporary command of the Black Pearl. By articulating his value proposition and aligning Barbossa's goals with his own, he illustrates the importance of finding common ground and leveraging mutual interests during negotiations.

In "Dead Man's Chest," Jack must convince his crew to embark on a peril-ous quest to locate the Dead Man's Chest. Crew members are initially hesi-tant to embark on the journey due to the danger involved. Through effective communication, Jack conveys the stakes and potential rewards of the quest. Using storytelling and his charismatic presence, he paints a vivid picture of the adventure, rallying the crew. While balancing honesty and motivation, Jack explains the risks transparently. It is important that he addresses the crew's concerns and frames the risks as challenges that can be overcome in order to ensure that everyone understands their roles and the potential outcomes.

Throughout "At World's End," the Pirate Lords must unite against the com-mon threat posed by their biggest enemy. As one of the Pirate Lords, Jack Sparrow plays a crucial role in the negotiations. As a Pirate Lord, Jack uses his influence and persuasive abilities to bring together diverse and often con-flicting interests. To preserve their way of life, he emphasizes the existential threat they face and the necessity of unity. Using his leadership skills to build consensus and broker compromises in complex political dynamics, Jack excels at navigating complex political dynamics. During high-stakes negotiations, his ability to articulate the benefits of collaboration and address the concerns of each Pirate Lord underscores the importance of effective communication. Jack Sparrow illustrates the advantages of collaboration by highlighting the immi-nent threat their enemy poses to their way of life, making it clear that individ-ual efforts will not be enough to overcome this threat. He convinces them that their freedom and autonomy can only be preserved by uniting their strengths and resources. In convincing the Pirate Lords to set aside differences and work together, Jack skillfully addresses each Lord's concerns while demonstrating how their cooperation serves both the collective and personal interests.

Leaders can learn more about persuasion and negotiation by examining Jack Sparrow's communication strategies. Modern leadership requires these skills to ensure that stakeholder engagement, information sharing, and align-ment are achieved.

Agility: Adaptability and Flexibility

Jack Sparrow's adventures in the "Pirates of the Caribbean" series highlight his exceptional agility, adaptability, and flexibility. He can adapt quickly to changing circumstances, such as shifting alliances and new threats. Leadership requires the ability to adapt quickly to changing circumstances and new risks. Whenever Jack is faced with a new situation, he applies the lessons he has learned from past experiences. Leaders should constantly learn from their past experiences and apply those lessons to their future endeavors.

As Jack Sparrow escapes from a life-threatening situation "The Curse of the Black Pearl," his agility and adaptability are evident. Jack uses available resources, such as ropes and pulleys of docked ships, to outmaneuver his pursuers when cornered on the dock. As a result of his ability to think on his feet in high-pressure situations and adapt, he demonstrates the importance of flexibility. A key component of Jack's success in the climax of "The Curse of the Black Pearl" is his ability to adapt to Barbossa and the cursed crew. As Jack shifts his strategy multiple times, he alternates between negotiating with Barbossa and fighting him. To even the odds, he uses the curse's rules to his advantage, temporarily becoming undead. Based on the dynamics of a situation, strategies must be adjusted accordingly.

In "Dead Man's Chest," Jack navigates a series of shifting alliances. Despite their conflicting interests, he forms a temporary truce with Will Turner and Elizabeth Swann. Jack's flexibility in dealing with different characters, including his handling of Davy Jones and his crew, demonstrates that leaders must adapt their approaches according to their stakeholders. The fact that he is willing to switch allegiances to achieve overarching goals emphasizes the importance of staying flexible.

As Jack faces the overwhelming force of the powerful enemy in "At World's End," he must adapt. In order to form a united front, he collaborates with former enemies and new allies, including Pirate Lords. The ability of Jack to pivot from a personal goal to a collective cause illustrates the importance of flexibility in leadership. As a result of this adaptability, he remains a key player in the fight against a common enemy.

The crew of Jack's ship is threatened by mermaids in "On Stranger Tides." His quick thinking and adaptability are evident as he devises an effective plan to capture a challenging target by creatively utilizing available resources. Leadership requires flexibility in problem-solving, as Jack had to switch from defensive maneuvers to a proactive approach in this situation.

In "Dead Men Tell No Tales," Jack faces very dramatic problem. Under extreme pressure, Jack demonstrates his ability to adapt his strategy on the fly and think creatively as he quickly improvises in a critical situation.

He communicates with his crew to coordinate a rescue, using chaos to his advantage. The importance of maintaining composure and adjusting to life-threatening changes quickly is underscored by this moment.

Jack Sparrow provides leaders with a valuable lesson in adapting to new circumstances, learning from past mistakes, and remaining flexible in the face of new risks. Emulating Jack's adaptability can help leaders navigate uncertainties, respond to evolving challenges, and guide their organizations to sustained success.

Problem-solving: Creative and Critical Thinking

Jack's innovative escape plans throughout the "Pirates of the Caribbean" series demonstrate his exceptional problem-solving abilities. Managing risks and addressing challenges requires creative solutions from leaders. Jack can determine the best course of action for each situation by analyzing situations from multiple perspectives. Leadership requires leaders to analyze situations from a variety of perspectives = to determine the best course of action. His creative and critical thinking abilities, risk assessment, and innovative solutions highlight essential problem-solving skills essential to effective leadership. These skills will enable leaders to navigate uncertainty, overcome challenges, and lead their organizations successfully.

When Jack Sparrow is captured and imprisoned in Port Royal in "The Curse of the Black Pearl," he must devise a plan to escape. Using his knowledge and resourcefulness, he analyzes the environment and uses improvised tools to escape. Through a series of calculated moves, Jack tricks the guards and uses the chains in his cell to his advantage. A leader facing unforeseen challenges must be able to think quickly and adapt to their surroundings.

Jack and his crew must outwit the Kraken, a monstrous sea creature, in "Dead Man's Chest." Jack's problem-solving skills manifest themselves as he devises creative strategies to use the ship's resources against overwhelming threats. By utilizing available tools in innovative ways, he can confront formidable challenges swiftly and effectively. By understanding the creature's behavior, he exploits its weaknesses. Rather than fully exploiting the Kraken's weaknesses, these tactics may have been more about delaying the inevitable. Even in the face of seemingly hopeless situations, his actions serve to buy time and protect his crew, showing his resourcefulness and willingness to face the creature head-on. Leadership can be inspired by Jack's ability to analyze a threat and develop a multifaceted approach to neutralize it.

In "At World's End," Jack must unite the Pirate Lords to confront a powerful and oppressive force threatening their way of life. He employs his problem-solving skills by leveraging his knowledge of each Lord's motivations and fears. In the negotiations, Jack successfully brings together the disparate factions by playing on their individual interests. Finding common ground and understanding diverse perspectives are key to achieving a collective goal. In the same film, Jack and his crew must find a way out from a trap. Using advanced navigation techniques and ancient seafaring traditions, Jack combines science and folklore to achieve his goals. Jack guides the ship back to reality by combining celestial navigation and brethren court stories. He illustrates the importance of integrating different approaches to solving complex problems through the integration of practical knowledge and abstract thinking.

In "On Stranger Tides," Jack also faces the formidable British Navy led by Captain Barbossa. As a captive, Jack influences his captors with his wit and charm, maximizing his chances of escaping. He convinces them that he can lead them to achieve their goals, only to orchestrate a daring escape. A disadvantageous situation can be turned into an opportunity by thinking quickly and turning a disadvantageous situation into a positive one.

Last but not least, Jack confronts Captain Salazar and his ghostly crew in "Dead Men Tell No Tales." Using his cunning and resourcefulness to turn the situation in his favor, Jack devises a plan to trap his formidable opponent. His knowledge of the supernatural and the environment allows him to create a scenario where Salazar's curse can be used against him. Utilizing unique insights and turning an opponent's strengths into weaknesses is a powerful strategy.

Like Captain Jack Sparrow, leaders who develop and hone these skills will be more capable of identifying, assessing, and mitigating risks, ensuring their organizations' success and stability.

SUMMARY

This chapter explored how risk management is crucial for organizational sustainability, stability, and success, requiring leaders to navigate various risks proactively. It also highlights the importance of understanding interdependencies, protecting assets, enhancing decision-making, fostering resilience, building trust, and developing essential skills such as analytical thinking, decision-making, communication, agility, and problem-solving.

Specifically, we considered the following:

- Leaders must navigate risks from market fluctuations, regulatory changes, technological advancements, and operational inefficiencies.

- Effective risk management builds organizational resilience.

- Leaders can prepare teams for crises and maintain operational continuity.

- Leaders who develop risk management skills can effectively identify, assess, and mitigate risks, ensuring organizational success and stability.

- Effective risk management helps leaders identify, assess, and mitigate risks, ensuring their organizations' long-term stability and success.

We conclude our discussion on risk management by exploring Captain Jack Sparrow's adventurous strategies. The next chapter highlights strategic planning as a skill to navigate uncharted waters, drawing parallels between corporate leaders and the infamous pirate as they chart courses toward long-term goals amidst uncertainties.

11

SAILING INTO THE FUTURE

"Pirates of the Caribbean" provides critical leadership lessons about strategic planning, which involves charting a course through uncharted waters. Strategic planning involves setting long-term goals and defining a roadmap to achieve them (Simerson, 2011), just as Captain Jack Sparrow meticulously plans his adventures. It begins by understanding the external and internal environments, much like a pirate must know the seas and their ship's capabilities.

Environmental scanning is the first step in strategic planning, which involves gathering and analyzing information about external factors that may impact the journey. Pirates would also assess weather patterns, potential threats from other ships, and opportunities for plunder.

Understanding the environment is the first step in formulating a strategy. Pirates would develop strategies to leverage their strengths, exploit opportunities, mitigate weaknesses, and avoid threats. In order to avoid naval patrols, it might be necessary to choose the right time to attack a well-guarded treasure fleet. In a business context, this involves defining corporate, business, and functional strategies. A corporate strategy might involve decisions about diversification and acquisitions, a business strategy might focus on cost leadership or differentiation, and a functional strategy might align resources within organizations to support the overall plan.

Putting plans into action follows strategy implementation. For pirates, this means executing their raid or voyage with precision, ensuring that every crew member knows their role. Organizations must align their structure, culture, and resources to support strategic initiatives. Leadership and communication play an important role in ensuring everyone is committed to the plan. Regular reviews and performance metrics help monitor progress and make necessary adjustments, just as a pirate captain would adjust course in response to changing conditions.

The final step of strategy evaluation is to assess success. Pirates would review their haul and tactics, learning from each voyage to improve their future efforts. Organizations use performance measurement tools, such as the balanced scorecard, to evaluate financial results, customer satisfaction, internal processes, and learning and growth. The use of continuous feedback and control mechanisms helps identify deviations and implement corrective actions, fostering a culture of continuous improvement.

As a result, strategic planning is an essential leadership skill, ensuring long-term goals are met while navigating uncertainties. In the pursuit of success, the Pirates of the Caribbean demonstrate the importance of thorough preparation, adaptive strategies, effective execution, and continuous learning.

STRATEGIC LEADERSHIP THEORY AND ITS RELATION TO STRATEGIC PLANNING

In strategic leadership theory, leaders are seen as change agents who can influence their organizations' strategy. It emphasizes the role of top executives and leaders in shaping and implementing strategies that drive organizational success. Creating a viable future for an organization requires strategic leadership, including the ability to anticipate, envision, maintain flexibility, and think strategically. The theory integrates different leadership styles and practices that are crucial to forming and executing strategies.

Strategic planning and strategic leadership are deeply intertwined. The process of strategic planning involves setting goals, formulating strategies, and outlining the steps needed to achieve them. Strategic leadership guides the planning process by providing vision, direction, and guidance.

The role of strategic leaders is crucial in gathering and interpreting information about external and internal environments. Using this information, they identify trends, opportunities, and threats that could affect the organization's strategy. Leaders use their vision and strategic thinking skills to develop comprehensive strategies. They ensure that the strategies align with the organization's vision, mission, and core values.

Additionally, strategic leaders foster a collaborative environment in which ideas and insights from various stakeholders are considered. Strategic leaders are key in transforming plans into action. They communicate strategy clearly to all levels of the organization, allocate resources efficiently, and ensure that the organizational structure supports the strategy. They also motivate and inspire employees to work toward achieving the company's goals.

Strategic planning requires continuous assessment and feedback. Strategic leaders monitor progress, measure performance against objectives, and make necessary adjustments to ensure the organization stays on track. They ensure that learning and improvement are integral parts of the strategic process.

Strategic leadership theory provides the basis for effective strategic planning. It ensures a dynamic, adaptable, and flexible planning process that can respond to changing environmental conditions. Leaders who demonstrate strategic leadership principles are better equipped to steer their organizations toward long-term success and sustainability.

STRATEGIC PLANNING STEPS

The "Pirates of the Caribbean" movie series shows how these strategic planning steps can lead to success on the high seas through spectacular adventures.

Preparation

For their quests to be successful, Captain Jack Sparrow and his crew prepare thoroughly before departing on their various dangerous missions and adventures. In "Pirates of the Caribbean: The Curse of the Black Pearl," Jack's meticulous planning is evident from the beginning. His escape from Port Royal was not a spur-of-the-moment decision but a well-thought-out plan involving several key steps.

The first thing Jack recognizes is that a ship is essential for any pirate, as it provides mobility and speed. By acquiring the Interceptor, one of the fastest ships in the fleet, he demonstrated his strategic thinking. As Jack understands, having the right vessel will provide a significant advantage in pursuits and escapes.

Recruitment is another vital component of Jack's preparation. In order to succeed in his endeavors, he carefully selects a capable crew whose skills and loyalty are paramount. For instance, he persuades Will Turner, a skilled swordsman and blacksmith, to join his crew, leveraging Will's desire to rescue

Elizabeth Swann. Jack ensures he has a competent ally by aligning Will's personal goals with his own.

Additionally, Jack gathers intelligence about his adversaries and potential obstacles as part of his preparation. He is well aware of the curse of the Black Pearl and its undead crew, which allows him to anticipate their moves and devise counterstrategies. His knowledge of the curse and his ability to use this information to his advantage exemplify strategic foresight.

Jack and his crew are well prepared to face the challenges that lie ahead as a result of this comprehensive preparation. It highlights the importance of having a clear plan, understanding one's resources, and adapting to unforeseen circumstances. As a result of Jack's careful preparation, he has enjoyed several successful escapades, demonstrating how good planning can lead to triumph even when the odds seem overwhelming.

Adaptive Strategies

In the "Pirates of the Caribbean" series, leading people consistently demonstrate the ability to adapt quickly to changing circumstances. This demonstrates the value of flexibility and quick thinking in strategic planning. Captain Jack Sparrow is particularly known for his quick adaptation and resourcefulness. In "Pirates of the Caribbean: Dead Man's Chest," Jack constantly adjusts his strategies to defeat his enemies. When confronted by the fearsome Kraken, for instance, he realizes that direct confrontation is pointless. Instead, he improvises with every new piece of information to avoid capture. This adaptive strategy allows Jack to survive and thrive in the face of unpredictable threats due to his ability to pivot and alter his plans on the fly.

Elizabeth Swann also shows remarkable adaptability. In "Pirates of the Caribbean: The Curse of the Black Pearl," Elizabeth uses her knowledge of naval protocol and her quick intellect to negotiate with Captain Barbossa, delaying her execution and buying time for rescue. Later, in "Pirates of the Caribbean: At World's End," she transitions from being a governor's daughter to becoming a pirate captain and eventually the Pirate King. Her ability to adapt to a variety of roles and environments illustrates the importance of flexibility and learning in leadership.

Similarly, Will Turner exemplifies adaptive strategies through his evolving skills and alliances. Will learns quickly to navigate the treacherous waters of piracy despite his limited experience as a blacksmith. In "Pirates of the Caribbean: Dead Man's Chest," he adapts by forming temporary alliances with unlikely partners like Jack Sparrow and even his former enemies to achieve his goals. The journey of Will from a law-abiding citizen to a savvy pirate shows how adaptability and the willingness to learn can lead to success.

Captain Hector Barbossa is another leader who embodies adaptive strategies. Having been resurrected by Tia Dalma, Barbossa quickly proves himself to again be a formidable leader, adapting to new circumstances and taking control of the Black Pearl once again. In "Pirates of the Caribbean: On Stranger Tides," he shifts his role from pirate captain to privateer under King George II, illustrating his ability to navigate politics as well as the seas.

As a result of their ability to adapt to changing environments and new challenges, all of them demonstrate the importance of adaptive strategies in leadership. In any adventure, whether it's Jack's cunning evasions, Elizabeth's strategic negotiations, Will's evolving alliances, or Barbossa's political maneuvering, you need flexibility, quick thinking, and the willingness to adjust your approach to overcome obstacles and seize opportunities.

Effective Execution

Pirates' success depends heavily on their ability to execute their plans, and the Pirates of the Caribbean series provides numerous examples of effective execution. In "Pirates of the Caribbean: At World's End," the alliance between pirates from different parts of the world demonstrates the effective execution of a unified strategy to eliminate the East India Trading Company. Their coordinated efforts in the final battle highlight the importance of executing a well-planned strategy to achieve their goals.

Jack's elaborate plan to retake the Black Pearl in "Pirates of the Caribbean: The Curse of the Black Pearl" is a great example of effective execution. By staging a mutiny, leveraging the cursed gold, and using clever deception, he managed to outmaneuver Captain Barbossa and regain control of the ship.

In "Pirates of the Caribbean: At World's End," Elizabeth's leadership plays a crucial role in uniting the pirate lords. Her ability to rally them and orchestrate a cohesive strategy against the East India Trading Company illustrates her effective diplomatic and strategic planning skills.

Will's determination to free his father, Bootstrap Bill, drives him to execute a daring plan to steal Davy Jones' heart in "Pirates of the Caribbean: Dead Man's Chest." Will demonstrates effective execution under pressure by sneaking aboard the Flying Dutchman and navigating its treacherous crew.

Barbossa's return from the dead and subsequent actions in "Pirates of the Caribbean: At World's End" demonstrate his ability to execute complex plans. As the leader of the charge to rescue Jack from Davy Jones' Locker, he plays a key role in the final battle, demonstrating his tactical prowess and leadership abilities.

In "Pirates of the Caribbean: At World's End," Tia Dalma's transformation into Calypso and her subsequent release are part of a grand plan to disrupt the balance of power. Despite the risks involved, the pirates' coordinated efforts to free her demonstrate the value of precise execution in achieving strategic goals.

Last but not least, Sao Feng, the Pirate Lord of Singapore, illustrates effective execution through his strategic alliances and tactical decisions. His alliance with the East India Trading Company and later shift to support the Brethren Court in "Pirates of the Caribbean: At World's End" demonstrate his ability to adapt and execute plans based on changing circumstances.

Throughout the Pirates of the Caribbean series, effective execution is a critical component to achieving strategic goals. Their success depends on their ability to execute well-planned strategies with precision and coordination, whether through intricate schemes, decisive leadership, or tactical maneuvers.

Continuous Learning

The "Pirates of the Caribbean" series emphasizes continuous learning, as pirates learn from their past experiences. This ability to learn and adapt from past experiences is crucial to their ongoing success.

Jack applies the lessons he learned from his previous adventures to outsmart Blackbeard to obtain his aims. He utilizes his knowledge of shipboard tactics and his experience manipulating other pirates to outwit Blackbeard and to achieve his goals. Using his strategic thinking and mastery of shipboard dynamics, Jack defeats Blackbeard by faking his cooperation while secretly orchestrating a plan to turn the tables. As a result of his continual learning and adaptability, Jack keeps one step ahead of his opponents.

Elizabeth's journey from a governor's daughter to the Pirate King is marked by constant learning. Using the skills and knowledge she acquired in previous films, such as diplomacy, combat, and leadership, she unites the pirate lords and leads the final battle against the East India Trading Company in "Pirates of the Caribbean: At World's End." The importance of continuous improvement is highlighted by her ability to learn and grow in the pirate world.

Will's transformation from a blacksmith to a skilled pirate and eventually the captain of the Flying Dutchman is also a testament to his continuous learning. In "Pirates of the Caribbean: Dead Man's Chest," Will uses his sword-fighting skills and knowledge of pirate codes to overcome challenges. As a result of his ability to adapt and learn from each encounter, he is more effective and more determined.

Barbossa's resurrection and subsequent actions in "Pirates of the Caribbean: At World's End" illustrate his ability to learn from past mistakes. Barbossa approaches his goals with greater cunning and strategic depth after experiencing betrayal and death. With each adventure, his knowledge of pirate lore and tactical acumen grow, making him an effective leader.

Even the infamous Davy Jones demonstrates learning through his encounters. As a result of past experiences, he modifies how he deals with enemies in "Pirates of the Caribbean: Dead Man's Chest," showing a keen understanding of both human nature (and pirate nature). He exploits the fears and weaknesses of those who cross him, such as using Will Turner's concern for his father to influence him into serving his interests. While his learning is often driven by revenge, it underscores the ongoing theme of adaptation and growth.

Tia Dalma learns that her power has limits and consequences when she is revealed to be the sea goddess Calypso. To achieve her goals, she adapts her approach to manipulating events and characters throughout the series. Through her interactions with others and her ability to learn from unfolding events, she highlights the mystical and strategic layers of continual learning.

"Pirates of the Caribbean" leaders demonstrate how continuous learning and adaptation are key to their survival and success. Reflecting on their past experiences, learning new skills, and adapting their strategies, the characters become increasingly competent and confident as they navigate the unpredictable and treacherous world of piracy.

The leaders in "Pirates of the Caribbean" demonstrate how preparation, adaptive strategies, effective execution, and continuous learning can lead to triumph even under the most dangerous conditions.

SUMMARY

Leaders can navigate uncertainties and achieve long-term success by incorporating the lessons of Pirates of the Caribbean into their strategic planning, preparation, adaptability, execution, and continuous learning. We considered the following:

- Leaders should understand both the external and internal environments before embarking on a mission. This will help them develop strategies for leveraging strengths, exploiting opportunities, mitigating weaknesses, and avoiding threats.

- Leaders should execute plans with precision, ensuring every team member knows their role. This can be done by reviewing outcomes and learning from each mission to improve future efforts.

- Leaders should recognize essential resources and potential obstacles. Preparation is the key to success, involving meticulous planning and resource alignment.

- Leaders should adapt to changing circumstances and seize new opportunities by transitioning smoothly between different roles and environments.

- Leaders should execute a unified strategy with precise coordination and clear roles. Strong leadership and strategic planning drive successful execution.

- Leaders should reflect on past experiences to improve future strategies and actions. Continuously develop new skills and deepen understanding, so leaders should also adapt approaches based on learned experiences to achieve better outcomes.

Building on strategic planning, we shift focus to crisis management, essential for navigating high-stakes situations. Leadership requires anticipating crises and reacting quickly. The next chapter examines crisis management, emergency preparation, and effective leadership under pressure, preparing leaders for turbulent times.

12

STORMY SEAS

There are no escaping crises in the world of leadership. Leaders often encounter unforeseen challenges and rough seas, just like the intrepid pirates in the film series "Pirates of the Caribbean." Yet, it is precisely during these times of adversity that true leadership emerges. We will examine how the pirates' strategies and resilience can be applied to crisis management in the real world.

VISIONARY LEADERSHIP

To be a visionary leader, you have to be able to create and articulate a realistic, credible, and compelling vision of the future that builds upon and improves on what is already in place (Kouzes & Posner, 2017). By maintaining focus on long-term objectives while adapting to immediate challenges, visionary leaders guide their teams through uncertainty and adversity.

ELEMENTS OF VISIONARY LEADERSHIP IN CRISIS MANAGEMENT

Clarity of Vision

In times of crisis, visionary leaders provide direction and purpose by articulating a clear and compelling vision. While other people find Captain Jack Sparrow's methods eccentric or risky, he often displays a clear vision, such as his relentless

pursuit of the Black Pearl. By focusing on the ultimate goal, such as retrieving
the Black Pearl, he provides his crew with a sense of purpose and direction.

Adaptability and Flexibility

In a crisis when situations can shift rapidly, visionary leaders are adaptable
and open to change. As a result of his flexibility, Jack Sparrow can adjust his
plans when faced with unexpected challenges, such as changing alliances or
unforeseen obstacles. As a result of his adaptability, he has been able to keep
moving toward his vision despite setbacks.

Inspiration and Motivation

Visionary leaders inspire and motivate their teams by communicating their
vision effectively and by leading by example. Even in dire situations, Jack
Sparrow's charisma and confidence inspire his crew to take bold actions.
While Captain Jack Sparrow was mutinied against, he was able to overcome
crises due to his ability to inspire loyalty at key moments and motivate his
crew in desperate situations.

Strategic Thinking and Innovation

A visionary leader uses innovation and strategic thinking to find creative
solutions to complex problems in a crisis. Sparrow uses unconventional
strategies and innovative thinking to overcome challenges, such as using the
undead curse to his advantage or escaping from impossible situations.

Resilience and Persistence

Leaders with vision demonstrate resilience and persistence, maintaining
focus on their vision despite obstacles. The resilience of Jack Sparrow can be
seen in his relentless pursuit of his goals, whether it's reclaiming his ship or
escaping capture. He serves as a powerful example of how visionary leadership can help navigate crises in the face of adversity.

Crisis Management

The process of crisis management involves identifying, assessing, and responding to unexpected events that threaten the stability and objectives of an organization or group. It requires a combination of strategic thinking, decisive action, and adaptability to navigate the complexities and uncertainties that arise during a crisis (Crandall et al., 2013).

LEADERSHIP STRATEGIES TO MANAGE CRISIS

Preparedness and Anticipation

Preparedness is the cornerstone of crisis management, similar to pirates anticipating attacks or confrontations. Leaders must adopt scenario planning to prepare for potential crises, envisioning a range of possibilities and formulating contingency plans. Similarly, resource readiness is crucial. Leaders should ensure their teams are well-equipped with tools, information, and support to handle crises effectively, just as pirates stockpile resources and secure allies before undertaking risky ventures.

Rapid Assessment and Decision-making

Rapid assessment and quick decision-making are also essential to effective crisis management. Leaders can take a cue from characters like Captain Jack Sparrow, who excels at quickly assessing situations and prioritizing key information to make informed decisions. Whether leaders have limited information or a lot of information, they must be able to act decisively. Leadership requires agility, which Sparrow demonstrates by making bold decisions to seize opportunities or avert disasters.

Communication and Coordination

During a crisis, effective communication is essential. As pirate crews coordinate efforts to manage threats, leaders must ensure seamless information flow among team members and stakeholders. Through strategic persuasion and shared goals, Captain Jack Sparrow managed to overcome crisis after crisis as he effectively communicated his vision, inspired loyalty when needed, and leveraged the strengths of his crew while facing mutiny. To achieve shared objectives, it is also essential to coordinate across different teams and stakeholders similar to pirates forming alliances.

Adaptability and Flexibility

Leaders often need flexibility and flexibility during crises, as well as dynamic problem-solving skills. Leaders should adapt their strategies to changing circumstances, emphasizing the importance of being open to new approaches and creative solutions. Despite setbacks, Jack Sparrow's perseverance in the face of adversity illustrates the importance of resilience and recovery.

Staying Calm Under Pressure

During a crisis, leaders must remain calm under pressure. It is normal for emotions to run high in such situations, but leaders must keep their composure and make rational decisions. Staying calm enables leaders to think clearly, assess situations objectively, and make sound decisions. The ability to stay calm under pressure inspires confidence in the team and aids them in navigating through the crisis. Jack Sparrow exemplifies this by remaining composed during moments such as navigating the Black Pearl through a violent storm or facing powerful enemies such as Davy Jones. He remains calm despite the chaos around him, making rational decisions, and inspiring confidence in his crew, guiding them through the crisis with great success.

Leading Through Uncertainty

Crises are characterized by uncertainty, and leaders must navigate them with confidence. It is important for leaders to provide their teams with a sense of stability and direction during times of uncertainty. Keeping everyone informed requires open communication, addressing concerns, and providing regular updates. Even in the face of uncertainty, leaders can inspire their team to stay focused and motivated by demonstrating resilience and adaptability. In chaotic situations like the battle against the Kraken, Jack Sparrow keeps his crew informed and focused. During uncertain and dangerous times, his resilience and ability to inspire confidence maintain stability and motivate his crew.

Learning and Reflection

As a final point, post-crisis evaluations are essential for continuous improvement. In the same way that pirates learned from their encounters and adjusted their tactics for future challenges, leaders should analyze what worked and what didn't. Jack Sparrow and his crew adapt their tactics after facing the Kraken. Their initial defeat forces them to reassess their approach, and they ultimately devise a new plan to confront the formidable creature, demonstrating their ability to learn from past experiences to improve future outcomes. In much the same way that pirates share wisdom and tactics to enhance their collective success, the collective becomes more resilient over time as these lessons and best practices are shared within the organization.

Leadership requires crisis management skills, and "The Pirates of the Caribbean" offers valuable lessons in navigating stormy seas. By embracing adaptability, building a resilient crew, communicating effectively, staying calm under pressure, leading through uncertainty, fostering innovation, and learning from mistakes, leaders can successfully navigate through crises and emerge stronger than ever. As with pirates, leaders must embrace uncertainty, face challenges head-on, and chart a course to success.

ESSENTIAL LEADERSHIP QUALITIES DURING CRISES

Strategic Alliances

As shown in "The Curse of the Black Pearl," Jack Sparrow, Will Turner, and Commodore Norrington formed an unlikely alliance against Captain Barbossa. It illustrates how factions with divergent goals can unite to defeat a common enemy. Their collaboration allows them to leverage their unique strengths and compensate for each other's weaknesses, which is crucial in crisis situations that require multifaceted solutions.

Quick Thinking and Adaptability

When Jack Sparrow arranges his risky escape in the movie series symbolizes the traits of effective leadership, such as quick thinking and adaptability. Sparrow's creative use of available resources to evade capture, such as improvising a sinking boat, illustrates the importance of resourcefulness and creativity in crises. He teaches leaders the importance of adaptability when conventional methods fail as a result of his ability to think on his feet and use his surroundings to his advantage.

Focus and Adaptation in Chaos

During the battle in "At World's End," there is a literal whirlpool known as the maelstrom, symbolizing the chaotic and unpredictable environments leaders often face. As the battle progresses, the characters must remain focused on their goals while adapting to a rapidly changing environment. Leaders can manage effectively by maintaining clarity of purpose and being flexible enough to adjust tactics as circumstances change. The ability to steer through chaos, not only by responding to immediate threats but also by keeping an eye on the long-term, is essential.

The examples from "Pirates of the Caribbean" demonstrate that effective leadership requires the ability to forge strategic alliances, think quickly, and adapt strategies on the fly. Each example illustrates how to navigate the tumultuous waters of leadership in any high-stakes environment. The skill and determination of leaders in today's dynamic world must be matched by the skill and determination of pirates who navigate unpredictable seas.

Leveraging Diverse Strengths

Another crucial lesson is the value of leveraging diverse strengths. Many of Jack Sparrow's successes are achieved through the collective skills of his crew members. Each member contributes a unique set of skills that Sparrow uses to navigate challenges, much as effective leaders enrich problem-solving and creativity through diverse perspectives and skills. In "Dead Man's Chest," Sparrow's crew's unique skills enable him to escape traps and outmaneuver enemies.

Elizabeth Swann goes from being a governor's daughter to becoming a pirate and a leader in her own right. While she often finds herself in unpredictable and dangerous situations, she manages to navigate them with confidence and cunning by embracing uncertainty. Her role as the Pirate King is pivotal in "At World's End," where she unites the pirate lords to fight against the East India Company. To defeat a common enemy, Elizabeth uses the combined forces and disparate strategies of the pirate lords to form a cohesive battle plan.

Balancing Short-term and Long-term Goals

Leaders should understand the importance of balancing short-term and long-term goals. Sparrow is adept at handling immediate crises while maintaining focus on his ultimate goal, whether it is finding a treasure or securing his freedom. When he negotiates with other pirates or navigates complex situations that require both immediate action and long-term strategy, he exemplifies this dual focus, as he did when dealing with the East India Trading Company, where he had to manage immediate threats while plotting for his long-term survival.

Achieving long-term goals while balancing immediate challenges is one of Will Turner's strengths. As he attempts to rescue Elizabeth, his motivations evolve into a broader quest that involves his father and the mystical elements of the pirate world. His decision to use the heart of Davy Jones serves both his immediate need to save himself and his friends as well as his long-term goal of freeing his father. This balancing act demonstrates his foresight and strategic thinking in crisis management.

Being Resourceful and Adaptative

Captain Hector Barbossa demonstrates resourcefulness and adaptability to changing circumstances. His return from the dead in "Dead Man's Chest" and subsequent alliances and betrayals demonstrate his strategic thinking and adaptability. His ability to navigate shifting allegiances within the pirate world, as well as his ability to survive seemingly insurmountable odds, shows Barbossa's ability to utilize whatever resources are at his disposal. He demonstrated his ability to leverage opportunities in chaos in "At World's End" through the negotiation with the enemy.

There is a lot to learn about crisis management from Pirates of the Caribbean. Today's dynamic environments require leaders to be resilient, strategically astute, and unwavering in their commitment to their goals, like the intrepid pirates who navigate the unpredictable seas. To navigate their ships successfully through the stormy waters of their professional and personal lives, current and aspiring leaders should adopt these qualities.

SUMMARY

We discussed the importance of having a clear and compelling vision to guide teams through uncertainty. Crisis management involves identifying, assessing, and responding to crises with strategic thinking, decisive action, and adaptability. Effective leadership during a crisis, like navigating stormy seas, requires adaptability, strategic foresight, and a resilient mindset. The following are considered:

- Leaders must maintain focus on long-term objectives while adapting to immediate challenges.

- Visionary leaders articulate clear directions during crises. Adaptability and flexibility are essential in rapidly changing situations.

- Leaders inspire and motivate their teams even in dire situations.

- Leaders should use innovative approaches to solve complex problems.

- Leaders should focus on goals despite obstacles.

- Leaders prepare for potential crises through scenario planning and ensure resource readiness. Quick, informed decision-making is crucial.

- Ensuring seamless information flow and coordinating efforts across teams.

- Leaders should adjust strategies to suit changing conditions. Leaders should maintain their composure to make rational decisions.

- Leaders need to provide stability and direction in uncertain times.

- Post-crisis evaluation is crucial for continuous improvement.

The lessons from pirate leadership remain clear as we navigate from crisis management to our conclusion. In turbulent times, pirates' strategic agility and resolve offer a blueprint for bold, decisive action. Let's move forward, inspired by pirates' enduring legacy, to innovate and lead with courage and vision in the 21st century.

13

CONCLUSION

THE PIRATE'S LEGACY IN 21ST-CENTURY LEADERSHIP

Pirates of the Caribbean stories have captivated audiences with their thrilling adventures, memorable characters, and epic battles on the high seas. They offer insights into the nature of leadership beyond the spectacle and swashbuckling action. By examining the leadership styles and decisions of characters like Jack Sparrow, Hector Barbossa, Elizabeth Swann, and Will Turner, we uncover timeless principles that resonate with modern leaders facing their own turbulent waters.

Adaptability and resilience are two of the most enduring lessons from Pirates of the Caribbean. With his unorthodox methods and ability to think on his feet, Jack Sparrow exemplifies the necessity of remaining flexible in uncertain times. Leaders today must navigate an ever-changing landscape, adapting their strategies to meet new challenges and opportunities. For long-term success, perseverance and adaptability are crucial, as demonstrated by the pirates' resilience in overcoming seemingly impossible odds.

Similar to today's volatile and fast-paced business world, the high seas present an unpredictable and hostile environment. Leaders must be prepared to pivot their strategies in response to changing circumstances, just as Jack Sparrow adjusts his plans based on new information and evolving circumstances. In navigating the Black Pearl through a violent storm or escaping a seemingly impossible predicament, Jack shows how leaders must remain calm under pressure and think creatively to succeed. Success comes from the ability to adapt and remain resilient in the face of adversity.

Pirates of the Caribbean illustrates the value of strategic partnerships through the dynamic interplay of alliances and rivalries. Whether forming uneasy alliances with former enemies or rallying a diverse crew, the characters demonstrate that collaboration is essential for success. By building and maintaining strategic alliances, fostering teamwork, and leveraging the strengths of diverse groups, leaders can learn from these examples.

Strategic alliances were often the difference between life and death in the chaotic and competitive world of piracy. Jack Sparrow often seeks alliances to bolster his position and achieve his goals despite his individualistic tendencies. It is clear from his temporary partnerships with Hector Barbossa and other adversaries that it is important to put aside personal differences to reach a common goal. The importance of collaboration and teamwork in complex business environments is particularly relevant in the modern era. As leaders, it is crucial to cultivate strong relationships with key stakeholders, both inside and outside their organizations, to leverage the collective expertise and resources of the organization.

Throughout their adventures, the pirates face numerous ethical dilemmas that challenge their values and principles. Despite great personal risk, characters like Will Turner and Elizabeth Swann consistently demonstrate integrity and a strong moral compass. The actions of these leaders demonstrate the importance of ethical leadership in earning the trust and respect of others. In today's complex ethical landscapes, leaders must make decisions that uphold their values and promote a culture of trust and integrity.

Leadership is about more than just doing the right thing; it's about building trust and credibility. Will Turner's unwavering commitment to his principles, even when it puts him at odds with others or places him in danger, highlights the importance of maintaining integrity. His steadfast adherence to his values, whether it was in his quest to save his father or his loyalty to Elizabeth, serves as a model for modern leaders who have to make difficult decisions while remaining ethical. Leaders who demonstrate ethical behavior inspire loyalty and trust among their teams and stakeholders in today's world, where transparency and accountability are paramount.

Jack Sparrow's imaginative approaches to problem-solving and his ability to think outside the box highlight the importance of innovation in leadership. To drive progress and achieve their goals, leaders must embrace creativity and take calculated risks. Pirates' ability to devise clever solutions to daunting challenges serves as a powerful reminder that innovation and creativity are essential components of effective leadership.

Innovation is the lifeblood of progress and a key differentiator of businesses. Jack Sparrow's unorthodox methods, from his escape plans to his strategies for outwitting enemies, illustrate the importance of creative thinking. Leaders of the 21st century need to cultivate their willingness to take risks and their ability to see opportunities where others see only problems. Innovation and creativity can provide a competitive advantage in an era of rapid technological advancements and shifting market dynamics. To foster innovation within organizations, leaders must encourage their teams to experiment, take risks, and explore new ideas.

Taking care to assess risk and make strategic decisions is essential for pirates on their journeys, which are filled with danger and uncertainty. Jack Sparrow's ability to evaluate potential consequences and make informed choices, even in the most precarious situations, illustrates the need to balance risk and reward. Strategic decision-making requires leaders to evaluate risks and opportunities, aligning their long-term vision and goals with their decisions.

Effective risk management is a critical component of leadership. Jack Sparrow's actions are often high stakes, but he carefully weighs the risks and rewards before making decisions. Jack's strategic thinking emphasizes the need for leaders to be both prudent and bold when dealing with dangerous battles or forming alliances with rivals. Leaders must develop the ability to accurately assess risks and balance short-term gains with long-term goals. It requires a deep understanding of the organization's goals, the competitive landscape, and how decisions may affect the organization.

Our exploration of leadership lessons from "Pirates of the Caribbean" concludes by emphasizing the fact that these cinematic adventures transcend the screen. As in the age of sail and piracy, resilience, adaptability, strategic collaboration, ethical leadership, and innovation remain essential today.

Those who navigate the turbulent waters of business, politics, education, or any other field can draw inspiration from Jack Sparrow's tales. Leaders can chart their own course toward success by embracing the pirate's spirit of adventure, creativity, and determination, guiding their organizations through upcoming challenges and opportunities.

In the end, these pirates left us more than daring exploits and buried treasure; they left us enduring leadership principles that continue to inspire and guide us today. Let us take these lessons with us as we sail forward, using them to become better and more effective leaders. We can carry on the pirate's legacy by navigating our own high seas with wisdom, courage, and a bit of swashbuckling flair.

The "Pirates of the Caribbean" series teaches us that effective leadership requires more than just skill and knowledge; it requires character, courage, and a willingness to embrace the unknown. By incorporating these lessons into our leadership practices, we can navigate the complexities of our modern world with the same boldness and ingenuity that defined the legendary pirates of the Caribbean. Our voyage to new horizons can be guided by timeless wisdom found in these iconic stories.

SUMMARY

Throughout this chapter, we examined how the "Pirates of the Caribbean" series teaches leadership lessons through adaptability and strategic alliances. Success can be achieved by navigating challenges with resilience, creativity, and integrity. Today's complex and dynamic environments require leaders to draw inspiration from these principles.

We considered the following:

- Leaders should recognize the necessity of remaining adaptable and resilient in the face of uncertainty and change.

- Collaboration and teamwork are essential for achieving common goals and navigating complex environments.

- Ethical leadership is crucial for building trust and credibility with teams and stakeholders.

- Embracing creativity and taking calculated risks are key to progress.

- Strategic decision-making requires careful consideration of both short-term gains and long-term goals.

- The pirates' enduring lessons of resilience, adaptability, strategic collaboration, ethical leadership, and innovation should inspire leaders. These principles remain relevant in guiding organizations through today's challenges.

- The leaders of today must embrace the spirit of adventure and creativity as they navigate the complexities of the modern world.

APPENDIX 1: PIRATES OF THE CARIBBEAN CHARACTERS

Character	Brief Description
Barbossa	A cunning and ruthless pirate captain who initially serves as the antagonist in the first film. He is known for his distinctive voice and love for apples. Barbossa is both a rival and an occasional ally to Jack Sparrow.
Blackbeard	Blackbeard, also known as Edward Teach, is one of the Caribbean's most feared and ruthless pirates. Using dark magic, Blackbeard controls his ship and crew and is obsessed with finding the Fountain of Youth to escape his prophesied end. His mastery of voodoo and formidable combat skills make him one of the series' most dangerous characters.
Carina Smyth	She is a highly intelligent and resourceful astronomer. She possesses a diary left to her by her father, which she believes holds clues to finding the Trident of Poseidon, an artifact of immense power.
Davy Jones	The legendary and fearsome captain of the Flying Dutchman, cursed to ferry the souls of those who die at sea. He is bound to the sea by a tragic love story and possesses a heart locked away in the Dead Man's Chest.
Elizabeth Swann	The adventurous and independent daughter of the Governor of Port Royal. Elizabeth is initially drawn into the world of piracy through her love for Will and her fascination with pirates, eventually becoming a formidable pirate in her own right.
George II	Great Britain's ruling monarch in the 18th century. He is known for his authoritative, impatient, and arrogant demeanor. King George II seeks to find the Fountain of Youth before rival powers, demonstrating his power-hungry nature and willingness to employ ruthless methods.
Gibbs	Jack Sparrow's loyal first mate and trusted confidant. Gibbs provides comic relief and valuable pirate lore throughout the series.
Jack Sparrow	A flamboyant and cunning pirate known for his quick wit, charm, and unorthodox methods. He is the former captain of the Black Pearl and often finds himself entangled in supernatural adventures.

(*continued*)

Character	Brief Description
James Norrington	He is a commodore in the Royal Navy. Norrington is depicted as a disciplined and honorable officer with a strong sense of duty. He is a rival to Captain Jack Sparrow and has complicated romantic feelings toward Elizabeth Swann, adding to the dynamic interplay between the characters.
Tia Dalma/Calypso	A mysterious and powerful voodoo priestess with knowledge of the sea and its magic. She is later revealed to be the sea goddess Calypso, bound in human form by the pirate lords.
The Kraken	The Kraken is a mythical sea creature. It is depicted as a massive, squid-like monster that serves Davy Jones, the supernatural captain of the Flying Dutchman. The Kraken is a symbol of Jones' power and his ability to control the seas, used primarily to destroy ships and drag them into the depths.
Weatherby Swann	He is the Governor of Port Royal and the father of Elizabeth Swann. Governor Swann is depicted as a dignified and well-meaning official who tries to navigate the dangerous waters of piracy while maintaining his duty to the Crown.
Will Turner	A skilled blacksmith and the son of pirate Bootstrap Bill Turner. Will is brave, loyal, and often driven by a sense of duty and love for Elizabeth Swann. Throughout the series, he evolves from a civilian into a skilled pirate.
Salazar	Salazar is cursed and transformed into a ghostly form, imprisoned in the Devil's Triangle with his ghostly crew of sailors. He hates all pirates, especially Jack Sparrow, whom he blames for his cursed fate. Because of his desire for revenge on Sparrow, Salazar possesses supernatural abilities that make him an extremely formidable and terrifying foe.

Pirates of the Caribbean characters mentioned in this book in alphabetical order.

APPENDIX 2: PIRATES OF THE CARIBBEAN MOVIES

Title	Format	Release Year	Description
Pirates of the Caribbean: The Curse of the Black Pearl	Movie	2003	This film introduces Captain Jack Sparrow, who is on a quest to retrieve his ship, the Black Pearl, from the cursed crew led by Captain Barbossa. Alongside him are Will Turner, a blacksmith, and Elizabeth Swann, the governor's daughter. The trio must break the curse that has doomed Barbossa and his crew to live as undead beings.
Pirates of the Caribbean: Dead Man's Chest	Movie	2006	Jack Sparrow discovers that he owes a blood debt to the legendary Davy Jones, captain of the ghostly Flying Dutchman. As Jones seeks to collect on this debt, Jack tries to avoid his fate while Will and Elizabeth find themselves caught up in Jack's misadventures once more, leading them to search for the Dead Man's Chest, which holds the heart of Davy Jones.
Pirates of the Caribbean: At World's End	Movie	2007	With the help of the resurrected Captain Barbossa, Will Turner and Elizabeth Swann attempt to rescue Jack Sparrow from Davy Jones' locker. They must then unite the pirate lords from around the world to fight against the East India Trading Company, which seeks to eradicate piracy with the help of Davy Jones.

(continued)

127

Title	Format	Release Year	Description
Pirates of the Caribbean: On Stranger Tides		2011	Jack Sparrow crosses paths with Angelica, an enigmatic woman from his past, who forces him aboard the Queen Anne's Revenge, the ship of the notorious pirate Blackbeard. They are all searching for the Fountain of Youth, facing challenges from the Spanish, and encountering mermaids along the way.
Pirates of the Caribbean: Dead Men Tell No Tales		2017	Jack Sparrow crosses paths with Angelica, an enigmatic woman from his past, who forces him aboard the Queen Anne's Revenge, the ship of the notorious pirate Blackbeard. They are all searching for the Fountain of Youth, facing challenges from the Spanish, and encountering mermaids along the way. The film follows Captain Jack Sparrow as he faces his old nemesis, Captain Salazar, who has escaped from the Devil's Triangle with his ghostly crew. Jack seeks the legendary Trident of Poseidon, a powerful artifact that grants its possessor total control over the seas, to defeat Salazar and save himself from certain doom.

Pirates of the Caribbean movies mentioned in this book.

REFERENCES

Adams, J. S. (1965). Inequity in social exchange. *Advances in Experimental Social Psychology, 2,* 267–299. https://doi.org/10.1016/S0065-2601(08)60108-2

Akpoviroro, K. S., Kadiri, B., & Owotutu, S. O. (2018). Effect of participative leadership style on employee's productivity. *International Journal of Economic Behavior (IJEB), 8*(1), 47–60.

Allende, S. C. (2018). *Be more pirate: Or how to take on the world and win.* Simon and Schuster.

Al-Zawahreh, A., & Al-Madi, F. (2012). The utility of equity theory in enhancing organizational effectiveness. *European Journal of Economics, Finance and Administrative Sciences, 46*(3), 159–169.

Assembly UN General. (1948). Universal declaration of human rights. UN General Assembly 302, no. 2: 14–25. United Nations. https://www.un.org/en/global-issues/gender-equality

Avolio, B. J., Bass, B. M., & Jung, D. I. (1999). Re-examining the components of transformational and transactional leadership using the multifactor leadership. *Journal of Occupational and Organizational Psychology, 72*(4), 441–462.

Baer, M. D., & Colquitt, J. A. (2018). *Why do people trust?: Moving toward a more comprehensive consideration of the antecedents of trust* (pp. 163–182). The Routledge Companion to Trust.

Barry, B., & Friedman, R. A. (1998). Bargainer characteristics in distributive and integrative negotiation. *Journal of Personality and Social Psychology, 74*(2), 345.

Bhattacharya, R., Devinney, T. M., & Pillutla, M. M. (1998). A formal model of trust based on outcomes. *Academy of Management Review, 23*(3), 459–472.

Brown, M. E., & Treviño, L. K. (2006). Ethical leadership: A review and future directions. *The Leadership Quarterly, 17*(6), 595–616.

Cambridge Dictionary. (n.d.). *Values.* Retrieved November 27, 2023, from https://dictionary.cambridge.org/dictionary/english/values

Conger, J. A., & Kanungo, R. N. (1987). Toward a behavioral theory of charismatic leadership in organizational settings. *Academy of Management Review, 12*(4), 637–647.

Cook, K. S., Cheshire, C., Rice, E. R., & Nakagawa, S. (2013). Social exchange theory. In *Handbook of social psychology* (pp. 61–88).

Cordingly, D. (2013). *Under the black flag: The romance and the reality of life among the pirates.* Random House.

Crandall, W. R., Parnell, J. A., & Spillan, J. E. (2013). *Crisis management: Leading in the new strategy landscape* (2nd ed.). Sage.

Dancy, J. R. (2015). *The myth of the press gang: Volunteers, impressment, and the naval manpower problem in the late eighteenth century.* Boydell Press.

DeFrank-Cole, L., & Tan, S. (2021). *Women and leadership: Journey toward equity.* Sage Publications.

Elliott, E. S., & Dweck, C. S. (1988). Goals: An approach to motivation and achievement. *Journal of Personality and Social Psychology, 54*(1), 5.

Fairhurst, G. T. (2005). Reframing the art of framing: Problems and prospects for leadership. *Leadership, 1*(2), 165–185.

Fairhurst, G. T. (2010). *The power of framing: Creating the language of leadership.* John Wiley & Sons.

French, J. R. P., & Raven, B. (1959). The bases of social power. In D. Cartwright (Ed.), *Studies in social power* (pp. 150–167). University of Michigan Press.

Hedges, L. (1990). Building winning teams: An interview with Charles Margerison and Dick McCann. *Executive Development, 3*(4). https://doi.org/10.1108/EUM0000000003828

Hopkin, P., & Thompson, C. (2021). *Fundamentals of risk management: Understanding, evaluating and implementing effective enterprise risk management* (6th ed.). Kogan Page.

House, R. J. (1976). *A 1976 theory of charismatic leadership.* Working Paper Series, 76-06.

Huitt, W. (2007). Maslow's hierarchy of needs. *Educational Psychology Interactive.* Valdosta State University, Valdosta. http://www.edpsycinteractive.org/topics/conation/maslow.html

Kellerman, B. (2004). *Bad leadership: What it is, how it happens, why it matters.* Harvard Business School Press.

Kets de Vries, M., & Cheak, A. (2015). Leadership in organizations, sociology of. In J. D. Wright (Ed.), *International encyclopedia of the social & behavioral sciences.* Elsevier. 10.1016/B978-0-08-097086-8.73080-7

Kouzes, J. M., & Posner, B. Z. (2017). *The leadership challenge: How to make extraordinary things happen in organizations* (6th ed.). Wiley.

Kuknor, S. C., & Bhattacharya, S. (2022). Inclusive leadership: New age leadership to foster organizational inclusion. *European Journal of Training and Development, 46*(9), 771–797.

Locke, E. A., & Latham, G. P. (2019). The development of goal setting theory: A half century retrospective. *Motivation Science*, *5*(2), 93.

Margerison, C., McCann, D., & Davies, R. (1986). The Margerison-McCann team management resource – Theory and applications. *International Journal of Manpower*, *7*(2), 2–32. https://doi.org/10.1108/eb045060

Marshall, R. (2011). *Pirates of the Caribbean: On stranger tides [Film]*. Walt Disney Studios.

Maslow, A. H. (1943). A theory of human motivation. *Psychological Review*, *2*, 21–28.

Merriam-Webster. (n.d.). *Trust*. Retrieved November 24, 2023, from https://www.merriam-webster.com/dictionary/trust

Micheli, P., Wilner, S. J., Bhatti, S. H., Mura, M., & Beverland, M. B. (2019). Doing design thinking: Conceptual review, synthesis, and research agenda. *Journal of Product Innovation Management*, *36*(2), 124–148.

Moniz, R. J. (2010). *History of managerial thought: A brief overview*. Practical and effective management of libraries, 1–18.

Montuori, A., & Donnelly, G. (2018). Transformative leadership. In *Handbook of personal and organizational transformation* (pp. 319–350). Springer.

Morgeson, F. P., Reider, M. H., & Campion, M. A. (2005). Selecting individuals in team settings: The importance of social skills, personality characteristics, and teamwork knowledge. *Personnel Psychology*, *58*(3), 583–611.

Nawaz, Z. A. K. D. A., & Khan, I. (2016). Leadership theories and styles: A literature review. *Leadership*, *16*(1), 1–7.

O'Keefe, B. J. (1988). The logic of message design: Individual differences in reasoning about communication. *Communications Monographs*, *55*(1), 80–103.

Patterson, K. A. (2003). *Servant leadership: A theoretical model*. Regent University.

Penney, S. A., Kelloway, E. K., & O'Keefe, D. (2015). *Trait theories of leadership*. Leadership in sport, 19–33.

Popper, M. (2004). Leadership as relationship. *Journal for the Theory of Social Behaviour*, *34*(2), 107–125.

Riggio, R. (2015). *Introduction to industrial and organizational psychology*. Routledge.

Rocheleau, D., Thomas-Slayter, B., & Wangari, E. (2013). *Feminist political ecology: Global issues and local experience*. Routledge.

Ryan, R. M., & Deci, E. L. (2000). Intrinsic and extrinsic motivations: Classic definitions and new directions. *Contemporary Educational Psychology*, *25*(1), 54–67.

SBCC. (2018). *SBCC and Gender Theories*. SBCC Implementation Kits. https://sbccimplementationkits.org/gender/sbcc-gender-theories/

Simerson, B. K. (2011). *Strategic planning: A practical guide to strategy formulation and execution.* Paraeger.

33rd Square. (2023). *Unpacking the pirate history and lore behind "parley".* Retrieved November 26, 2023, from https://www.33rdsquare.com/unpacking-the-pirate-history-and-lore-behind-parley/

Thompson, G., & Glasø, L. (2015). Situational leadership theory: A test from three perspectives. *Leadership & Organization Development Journal, 36*(5), 527–544.

Tuckman, B. W. (1965). Developmental sequence in small groups. *Psychological Bulletin, 63*(6), 384.

Tuulik, K., Õunapuu, T., Kuimet, K., & Titov, E. (2016). Rokeach's instrumental and terminal values as descriptors of modern organisation values. *International Journal of Organizational Leadership, 5,* 151–161.

Underdal, A. (1994). Leadership theory. In *International multilateral negotiation–approaches to the management of complexity* (pp. 178–197).

Verbinski, G. (2003). *Pirates of the Caribbean: The curse of the Black Pearl [Film].* Walt Disney Studios.

Verbinski, G. (2006). *Pirates of the Caribbean: Dead Man's Chest [Film].* Walt Disney Studios.

von Bertalanffy, L. (2015). *General system theory: Foundations, development, applications.* George Braziller Inc.

Wang, Q., Hou, H., & Li, Z. (2022). Participative leadership: A literature review and prospects for future research. *Frontiers in Psychology, 13,* 924357. https://doi.org/10.3389/fpsyg.2022.924357

www.ingramcontent.com/pod-product-compliance
Lightning Source LLC
Chambersburg PA
CBHW061255220326
41599CB00028B/5666